I THINK I SCARED HER:
GROWING UP WITH PSYCHOSIS

I THINK I SCARED HER:

GROWING UP WITH PSYCHOSIS

Growing Up With Psychosis

Brooke Katz

To order additional copies of this book, contact:
Xlibris Corporation
1-888-795-4274
www.Xlibris.com
Orders@Xlibris.com
23548

CONTENTS

Introduction 11

Chapter 1: Gym Lockers, Crayfish, and
  the Monkey Bars 13

Chapter 2: Anonymous Notes 29

Chapter 3: I Love to Sing 41

Chapter 4: How Teachers Make a Difference 53

Chapter 5: Saltines and Apple Juice 75

Chapter 6: Boston Calls 82

Chapter 7: Denied Again 94

Chapter 8: The Big Orange Pill 104

Chapter 9: I Think I Scared Her 115

Epilogue 123

Brooke Katz is a remarkable young woman, with an important and compelling story to tell, and she tells it well in her autobiographical book "Growing Up with Psychosis." Brooke draws the reader into a much misunderstood aspect of human existence and leaves us with an intensely personal sense of what it means and feels like to have a serious mental illness.

The subject of Brooke's book is provocative, as it involves her first hand experience with one of the few conditions still stigmatized in our culture. It is also timely, as the issues surrounding mental illness are beginning to receive more attention. A few years ago, then Surgeon General David Satcher estimated that one out of four adults and one out of five children suffer each year from a serious mental illness. The World Health Organization reports that psychiatric disorders are four of the ten leading causes of disability worldwide. We are all affected by these disorders, whether in ourselves or in our relatives or close friends. Yet few of us know the signs or symptoms of these illnesses. Few of us admit we have seen them in others or have them ourselves. Brooke describes them, their effect on her life, and her growing competence to understand and treat her illness in a style that makes her symptoms and her struggle clear to the professional and the lay reader alike. The result is a book which is intimate, frightening, deeply moving, and ultimately uplifting.

Others have written successful books on aspects of their own experiences with mental illness; William Styron on his depressions, Kay Jamison on her bipolar disorder and suicidality. However, no one has ever written this well on the most intriguing psychiatric condition of all, psychotic disorders, in which delusional thoughts and internal voices present themselves as real and compete with the world around us for attention.

Brooke's dramatic condition is one few of us know much about, though it fascinates many. We have all had her world misrepresented to us, from ancient times in myth and fairy tales, and in modern times in television and in the movies. We glimpse it, often through antiquated understandings and stilted presentations, in college textbooks of psychology. Brooke's story, the true story of living with psychosis, is one others should hear, and I believe it is a story many will want to hear.

Some books (such as *Uncle Tom's Cabin, Of Mice and Men, Catcher in the Rye*) change the way entire societies look at issues. This memoir may be one of those books.

I recommend this talented author and her book most highly to you.

Bruce M. Cohen M.D., Ph.D.
President, Psychiatrist in Chief McLean Hospital
Professor of Psychiatry Harvard Medical School

This extraordinary book reminds me how little we know and how much we can learn by looking through the patient's eyes. It is filled with passion, mystery, despair, hope and uncertainty . . . in a remarkable mix that enthralls and keeps the pages flying. Health professionals, patients, and everyone who feels well and thinks about those less fortunate will profit from reading this book carefully.

Tom Delbanco, M.D.
Koplow-Tullis Professor of General Medicine and Primary Care
Harvard Medical School and Beth Israel Deaconess Medical Center

INTRODUCTION

"No one knew that I was being followed and pursued, not even my friends or my parents. I was afraid that if I told my friends, *they* would want to kill the person I told because the person would know about *them* . . . So I didn't tell anyone. It was better for me to just keep it a secret."

—**Brooke Katz** regarding the voices that tormented her as a young girl—

This is a story about an extraordinarily courageous woman, Brooke Katz; the story involves her emergence from a life riddled with intrusive voices, paranoia, and confusion into a life brightly colored with her success as an honors college student and as "the most valuable player" on her lacrosse team. As a young girl, Brooke tried to live a normal life, go to school, play sports and have friends, while quietly suffering from an undiagnosed psychotic illness. In addition, she hid her symptoms from everyone, including her parents, friends and teachers.

The hallucinations (voices, visions), unusual thinking and anxiety that are all a part of a psychotic illness disorder are extremely disturbing for any one of any age to experience. When a child or adolescent is affected, their symptoms are often more pronounced than those seen in adults and more impairing, due to their early age of onset. Such symptoms often seriously interrupt a child's development at a critical time in life, when young minds and bodies are in the midst of a rapid growth spurt. Although relatively uncommon, psychosis does occur in children, in some, even before the age of 12 years; for example, schizophrenia occurs in about 1 out of 5,000 youths. These youths have high rates of suffering, substance abuse and suicide attempts. Everything in life is harder when a child's thinking is fragmented; for example, it is more difficult to concentrate in school, to be with and act friendly towards others, not to be overwhelmed with anxiety, not to believe that the unusual thoughts are true, not to pay attention to or act on what the voices say. Above all, it is extremely difficult to hide these deep, dark and disturbing thoughts from other people. Yet, many children and adolescents do hide their psychotic symptoms for years, while leading quiet tortured lives, just like Brooke, until the symptoms become so intense and frequent that they erupt and can no longer be hidden.

Brooke has had an incredible journey. She tells her story brilliantly, punctuated with humor and pain. The reader has a clear appreciation for the human being "behind" the mental illness and of what it must be like to walk through the world, viewing events through a psychotic window. Brooke describes her quest for obtaining the correct diagnosis, talks about her journey towards finding the best medication combination and ultimately, she describes her incredible healing process and successful reintegration into society.

I feel honored to know Brooke Katz. All individuals suffering from mental illness, their friends and their families should read her story. It is a story of hope, strength and courage; a story that demonstrates that there is and can be life after psychosis.

Jean A. Frazier, M.D.
Director, Pediatric Psychotic Disorders Program
Director, Child and Adolescent Psychiatry Outpatient Services
Assistant Professor of Psychiatry
McLean Hospital
Harvard Medical School

CHAPTER 1

Gym Lockers, Crayfish, and
the Monkey Bars

I looked around the corner. I didn't see anyone coming. I seized the opportunity and ran into the girls' bathroom. The heavy wooden door squeaked as I pulled it open. I put the hall pass on the ledge of the mirror and went into the third stall. Things that were multiples of three were the safest. Just as I finished and was about to flush I heard the door creak open. It was a fourth grader, one year older than me. Her body showed through the crack between my door and the yellow-painted stall next to mine. I couldn't let her see me; she might be one of *them*. I picked my feet up off the rubbery linoleum floor, and my black Converse sneakers rested on the edge of the toilet. Fear enveloped me; fear that the girl saw my hall pass. She knew I was in there. I had to get out before she called the rest of *them* in to get me. As soon as she started to pee I pressed the flusher three times and sprinted out the door, grabbing the hall pass on my way. I didn't even wash my hands. The hallway looked clear. The water fountain rinsed my hands, and then I rubbed them dry on my yellow sweat suit.

My friends wore jeans and blouses, but jeans were uncomfortable, and blouses are too girly, so I stuck with sweat suits and T-shirts. I walked into the big red square where all the classrooms were, and I went back into my third-grade classroom and sat down at my cluster. My friends would never understand what it's like to be chased. I didn't know why *they* were trying to kill me, but it was necessary to be careful not to go anywhere alone, or else *they* would kill me. Mrs. Finn, my teacher, was sitting at her desk, and everyone was working on their handwriting books. Mrs. Finn had medium-length gray hair, and she dressed like a teacher in long skirts and flowery tops. I wondered if she was one of *them*. She was always nice to me, but I couldn't be sure, she might be covering up.

No one knew that I was being followed and pursued, not even my friends or my parents. I was afraid that if I told my friends, *they* would want to kill the person I told because the person would know about *them*. If I told my parents, they would either not believe me (I knew my situation was peculiar), or they would take me away and hide me somewhere. Hiding me might be a good solution temporarily, but *they* were smart, and *they* would find me. *They* would be angry that I was hidden, so *they* would not only kill me, but *they* would torture me. So I didn't tell anyone. It was better for me to just keep it a secret.

I turned my handwriting book to the page on capital *G*, just like everyone else. Academically, I ruled. During math class they separated the thirty kids in my grade into three sections. I was in the top section, and my section met upstairs with Mrs. Adams. The walls were covered with math problems and posters that were academic and inspiring. I scored 100 percent on most of the tests. There was a boy in the class named Bill, and he was the only one who seemed smarter than I One day Mrs. Adams let us write our answers on the blackboard. This was fun, but my handwriting was awful. When I had to write in math class, I was disappointed. Every three months we got a report card; my marks were always "Excellent" except for handwriting, which consistently got a "Needs Improvement." I practiced my capital *G*s with conviction. I was determined to be perfect. I didn't know what I had done to make *them* need to kill me, but I definitely didn't want to do anything bad ever again. Just to be safe, I had to do everything perfectly. To the outsider, I was pretty close to perfect.

After handwriting came lunch. School lunches tasted bad, so

I brought my own. Every day I ate turkey and Muenster cheese on rye bread with a little bit of lettuce but no mayonnaise. I had to make my lunch myself because my mom didn't want me to be lazy. The hierarchy of school lunch tables made me angry, so I started a trend of pushing together two or three tables and sitting with a big group of friends. I went to a private school so there were only thirty people in my grade. If we pushed together three tables, everyone who wanted to could sit together. There were always a few people who were "too cool" (TC) to sit with everyone, and so they sat on their own.

Before the big-table idea, it was terrible. The same four girls and four boys sat together every day, and if someone else wanted to sit by them, they couldn't. The further the tables got from the snack bar, the less popular they were considered. When it was warm outside, everyone could sit outside on the lawn, but it was the middle of February, and it was cold in Princeton, New Jersey. Another beneficial aspect of eating outside was that when I got sent to lunch duty, it was easy to clean the cafeteria because no one ate there. Teachers sent me to lunch duty quite often.

My third-grade year started out with the classrooms rotating who cleaned up after lunch, but soon the administration realized that it would be better to punish kids by sending them to lunch duty. I was sent to lunch duty for things like throwing erasers at my friends, coming in late to class, and most commonly, talking back to the teachers. I had a big mouth for a nine-year-old girl. I told the truth, even when no one asked for it. I insulted people, mostly teachers, and I humiliated those who made even the smallest mistake in front of the class. I've always been taught that people who pick on others have low self-esteem. In my case, I didn't have self-esteem issues, I just wanted to be funny. I wanted to be the center of attention. I needed to be thought of as strong and bright. That way, no one could find out about *them* and how bad I really was. Maybe it was a self-esteem issue after all.

No matter what prompted my acting out, I got punished most of the time. Not even the slimy feeling of reaching into the bucket to grab a wet towel could deter me. The water rarely got cleaned, and the rags were gross. All I did for lunch duty was stand around with a rag in my hand, letting it drip onto the floor. All the other kids who were being punished wiped the tables vigorously, trying to get out in time to play some basketball before lunch ended. Immediately after lunch we had PE. I still want to know whose bright idea it was to have PE right after lunch. I loved PE. In PE we played dodge ball and practiced for the Presidential Fitness Test. I ran the shuttle run faster than any other girl, and I could hang from the chin-up bar forever. I was an athlete. My team always won in dodge ball.

There was one part of PE that eventually led me to fear PE. The locker room was the worst thing imaginable. I did not have to face it until fifth grade, but even now, in third grade, I walked through every once in a while and tried to tell myself that it wouldn't be that bad. Positive self-talk did not work though, I was terrified of the locker room. The thought of having to be with fifteen other girls, all naked and walking around, made me want to break my leg. Fortunately, I didn't have to worry about that yet because I had two years before I would have to wear a gym uniform.

Besides PE, my favorite subject was math. I liked problems that had an answer. With writing you couldn't really be right or wrong, you could only be good or bad. With math I was always right or wrong, and more often than not I was right. I think I was so strong in math because I was so competitive. Math gave me something to focus on. When I was sitting in the classroom, I was scared that at any moment everyone was going to take out a knife and start chasing me. *They* screamed at me. *"You're so stupid! You're going to die. You don't have any friends. None of your classmates like you. If you don't escape, they are going to kill you. You have no friends"*

But when I was doing math problems, I was able to concentrate on what I was doing, and I wasn't so scared. Both my brothers were good at math too, so some people say it runs in the family. My dad was a math major in college.

My older brother Ben was one year ahead of me in school.

He set the expectations with everything that he did. I had to do equally well or better—not because anyone said I have to—just because I was so competitive. Ben was just about perfect at age ten, so I had little room for messing up.

One time I got caught in science class killing the crayfish that we were supposed to be collecting and preserving. There were so many of them that I thought killing a few wouldn't make a difference. I'd go upstream from the rest of my class and pick the claws off of the crayfish one by one so they couldn't move. Then, once I had them all piled up, I took a rock and bashed it in their heads and poked out their eyes. After I had killed about twelve crayfish, I would throw them in the grass nearby. No one ever found them. Usually, I easily rejoined my class and completed the experiment. When the teacher caught me, he said, "You should never kill animals because they are living, just like us." I didn't care. I don't know why I killed the crayfish. Killing made me feel powerful and strong.

On the way back up to the school, we had to jump over the fence that marked the boundary of the school property. In the future I would become very familiar with this fence because that is where everyone would congregate to smoke. But for now, the fence was just a fun opportunity to watch all the other girls in tight jeans and skirts struggle to make it over the fence. In science class, when we weren't outside collecting samples, we got to do cool things like building bridges out of paper and then seeing how much weight they could hold. I made a paper-and-tape bridge that could hold the most weight of any of my classmates' bridges. I don't remember how I did it, but I remember it involved triangles. Science was fun.

At the end of the day we had recess, and I ran out to the playground. It was Thursday, which meant that I had about ten minutes to play before the van came to take us home. I swung upside down on the monkey bars and showed off my penny-drops. I had done it so many times I wasn't even afraid of landing on my head. My friends, Holly and Lee, followed me. We whispered secrets about who knows what. I loved school. I felt pretty safe there most of the time. I rarely had to be alone, and when I did, I could just make sure to do everything three times. That helped keep me safe.

Besides the monkey bars, the playground consisted of the soccer field, the baseball field, the six swings, the seesaws, the playhouse, and the climbing tree. We weren't allowed to climb higher than ten feet. My friends both left so I ran towards the house—a little wooden playhouse that was next to the climbing tree. I saw something shiny on the ground and picked it up. It was a screw, a sharp screw. I went into the house. Without thinking, I held the screw in my right hand and cut my lower left wrist with the screw. It wasn't a deep cut, just deep enough to bleed. It didn't hurt at all; it felt good. I felt a sensation of relief. It made me feel calmer inside my head.

I wasn't trying to kill myself, and I didn't want anyone to know what I had done. I went to the nurses' office, and the nurse asked what happened. I told her I fell and the metal bar on the monkey bars had a jagged edge that cut me. This was the first of many excuses to come. Eventually I tried excuses like "I got a paper cut on a piece of poster board," or "I was writing and my mechanical pencil slipped." I came up with some great excuses because I loved cutting myself, but I didn't want to get caught. I knew I'd get into trouble with the teachers and my parents. I was afraid of disease so I only cut myself with things that looked new and clean. At the time, I thought I was being cautious. The nurse treated me nicely, and she cleaned the cut and then put a big Band-Aid on it. I ran out to find the van waiting for me.

I thought a lot about how and why I cut myself. I took control of my emotions. I acted happy when I was actually scared and confused. I did this a lot, and it was getting to the point that at the same time as I took complete control, I lost my ability to feel. No matter what my body's response to something was, my brain gave a happy reaction. This was the only reaction my brain knew. I went home and then, as usual, went to soccer practice. I was on a select team called the YMS Express. The girls were mostly nice, but I only had one friend on the team—my next-door neighbor, Dara. Dara was a great soccer player. She was fast and strong. We often played on the same team. Dara and her sister Shelby were also my best friends. I had best friends at school and best friends at home. I spent all my free time with them. Anytime my family or their family went somewhere, we all tagged along. Dara and Shelby had toys like a giant erector set that we used to build forts with blankets. Then we played make-pretend house or school. They had a room that was all set up as a pretend kitchen; it even had a fake refrigerator and stove. There was another room in their basement set up with desks and a blackboard that we used as a school. I had so much fun, and I was safe at their house. I could even sleep over at their house without *them* trying to kill me. That was the only house I knew of that was so safe. I played with Dara and Shelby a lot.

Anyway, at soccer practice I ran around and played hard, hoping that I would feel tired and calmer afterwards. I was able to focus on soccer so well that no one knew anything was going on, not even Dara. I went home, took a shower, and did my homework. Then I played basketball with my dad and brothers. Phil was only five, and Ben was eleven, but I could beat both of them. Although Phil grew up to be quite an athlete, I was the only athletic one when we were younger. Sports was one area where Ben did not set the expectations for me because I was better than him.

Finally, it was time for bed. I wanted to cut myself again. I wanted that rush of calmness I got when I cut myself last time. But I was scared. I went to bed without any further self-harm. I woke up during the night with the worst stomachache in the world (although I'd had equally bad stomachaches the two previous nights). I woke my mom and dad up. "Mommy, my belly hurts." My talk became babyish when I needed help. They made a hot water bottle for me and gave me some Coke. More importantly, I took some Pepto-Bismol. I was addicted to Pepto. Every night I got a stomachache, and every night I took the Pepto It was a ritual. No one could figure out why I was getting stomachaches, but I knew.

I was scared that I was going to be killed in my sleep. The Pepto did not make my fears go away, but it did take the edge off my stomachache. I fell back asleep within an hour, and I woke up just before my alarm. I loved Fridays. Fridays meant extra recess, a stop at the deli on the way home from school, no homework, and I could usually go over to a friend's house after school or have a friend over. I sat up to find *them* staring in my window at me. *They* were three big men. *They* looked like oversized humans. There was one black man and two white men. *They* wore jeans and flannel shirts. *They* would have resembled construction workers if *they* weren't so big. *They* usually appeared in windows or open doorways. *They* carried guns sometimes, but this time *they* each had a big knife. I almost screamed, but I couldn't give up. I couldn't let anyone know my secret. Instead I went in to the bathroom where my brothers and Mom were getting ready. After brushing my teeth three times and washing my face three times, I couldn't waste any more time in the bathroom. I was going to have to go back into my room.

I didn't even have a weapon. I fumbled to find the light switch, and then when I looked up *they* were gone from my window. That could mean only one thing: *they* had entered my room. I froze. *They* could be in any drawer, closet, or empty space. I took my Swiss Army knife that I had stolen from a kid at school (my parents would never let me buy one), and I opened my underwear drawer. I went through each drawer that I needed until I was dressed. I wore my green sweat suit. Just as I closed the door behind me on my way out, I heard *them* yell, *"We'll get you, you bitch."*

I sprinted downstairs and ran into my mom who was holding my hairbrush. "I was just coming to get you, Brooke; it's time to do your hair." My hair was long and thick. When my mom made it into a ponytail, in stayed in place the best. I sat down and patiently let my mom make a ponytail. The five minutes that I sat in the wicker kitchen bar stool were the five calmest minutes of my day, every day. It was one of the few consistent things in my life. It was 6:45. The van usually came around at

6:50 a.m, so Ben and I sat by the window. "Beep, beep." The van was here. As we left, my mom tried to hug me. "Let go!" I screamed. I hated it when people touched me. I didn't know why.

My mom said, "Oh, just a little hug won't hurt you."

"No!" I demanded. I was not going to hug or touch anyone. I would shake hands, but that's about it.

I didn't hug anyone, not even my friends at school. Our family had a "no physical contact" rule where we couldn't touch each other. This was to avoid us hurting each other, but I think I got used to the "no touching," and I didn't know how to break it. Sometimes I felt like I wasn't real, and I thought if my mom tried to touch me she would stick her hand right through me and figure out that I wasn't really her daughter. Most of the time though, I just was disgusted by the thought of someone touching me. So I got on the bus without a hug. I sat in the back corner. My brother Ben sat in the front. I liked sitting near the older girls, next to the window.

The van ride was about thirty-five minutes, and I mostly just listened to people's conversations. When we got to school though, I was in for another day of adventures, just like most days. I had ten minutes before school was supposed to start, so I headed to the playground. We were supposed to go right to class because the playground wasn't supervised before school, but I didn't feel like it. I went back to see if I could find that screw I had cut myself with. Cutting myself made me feel safe from *them*. Cutting made me feel like no one was trying to kill me. Then I thought about disease. I didn't want to get a blood infection from using a dirty screw. I went into the playhouse, and I took out my black pen and pulled the metal clip off of it. It was sharp enough to cut me, but I'd have to press hard. I held the metal in my right hand and pulled up my left sleeve. I turned my wrist up and dragged the metal along the soft white part of my arm. The metal must have been sharper than I thought because blood started going everywhere. It wasn't a deep cut, but it was long. The blood was dark red, and I could see the gray part of the inside of my skin where the cut was. The blood rushed down my arm, and it felt warm. I could feel the cut pulsing. I saw an adult coming, and I ducked.

I thought I should be crying, but I didn't know how to cry. As a baby I must have cried, but I don't remember. The adult walked right by the playhouse and didn't see me. I pulled down my sleeve, and then *they* yelled at me. *"Die, die . . . you're so stupid, kill yourself, die, die"* *They* were quiet for a moment when I cut, but then *they* got angry. I knew *they* were angry because I'd almost got caught. I ran into the school building, and the first-grade teacher stopped me. I didn't know her name, but she knew mine. "Brooke, you're bleeding on your shirt," she whispered in my ear, trying not to embarrass me.

"I know," I told her. "What should I do?" She took me to the nurse. I blurted out some more lies about falling on an old screw, and she wrapped up my arm and sent me away. Now I had two cuts on my left arm. This new cut would require many lies. I was nervous that my mom wouldn't believe me, but I had the whole day to think of a good story for her.

I was late to class, and when I got there, everyone was writing in their journal. I pulled out my journal.

Dear Whoever Cares,

It feels like nobody cares, but I won't let anyone care so how are they supposed to? I don't know what to do. I am so scared because I am going to die before the end of the day. I can tell that it will be today. *They* are everywhere. I want to live. If I can't live, I at least want to have a chance to say goodbye to my friends. I hate keeping this such a big secret. *They* keep telling me to kill myself, but I don't want to kill myself. I'm so scared. If anyone finds out that I have been cutting my own arm they will send me away to a hospital for people who are crazy. Holly told me about how they put crazy people in straightjackets, and I don't want that. I'm not crazy, but there must be something wrong with me. I feel like I am just special because I am chosen, but I must have done something wrong. I can't figure anything out.

Brooke

The bell rang, and I realized what I had written. The teachers read these journals! I could be in huge trouble if they read what I wrote. I ripped it out and took my journal with me. During snack break I asked Holly what the journal topic had been, and she said, "Endangered species." I wrote a quick blurb on how people shouldn't hunt elephants and then threw my journal in the pile. No one would ever notice. I did keep a private journal at home, locked in a drawer to make sure the housekeepers never read it. In my private journal, I wrote about everything from the conspiracy to my soccer team. I liked to write.

After break was math time. I liked being with Mrs. Adams in the A group. Math was fun. We did problems in teams. Every month the teacher put a jar of candy out, and we got to "guesstimate" how many pieces of candy were in the jar. I had never won yet, but it was a fun game. *They* didn't bother me during math.

I had a good lunch—a turkey sandwich and Oreos—and then I headed back to the playground. My arm was bothering me, and I wanted to take the bandage off to see what the cut looked like. I left it on though, afraid it would still be bloody. At the water fountain I heard *"Stop!"* I paused only to hear *"You are a terrible person. You must die."* I started walking again, but *they* yelled at me. I thought I was going to die. *They* were going to murder me right there in the hallway. I crouched down into a fetal position and covered my ears. It didn't help, *they* were as loud as ever. I shut my eyes so people might think I was sleeping. Maybe *they* had poisoned my food. Maybe *they* were going to stab me to death with a magical knife that wouldn't make me bleed. I didn't know. I don't know how long I stayed still, curled up in that fetal position.

All of a sudden I felt like I had blinked and was back in my English classroom. I looked at the clock, and it was 2:50 p.m. About two hours had passed. I felt a little calmer, and I looked around at my friends. Holly sat next to me. I asked her if she wanted to come over after school and ride the van home with me. "Sure," she answered, "but I have to be home at six o'clock for gymnastics." Holly was a gymnastics ace. She had a trampoline in her backyard where she practiced flips. When the bell rang, I put away my English book, though I had no idea what chapter we were on. I ran out to call my mom to see if Holly could come over. My mom agreed, and Holly and I sat talking about what we would do that afternoon.

Finally the van came to take us home. It was Friday, so we got to stop at the deli and get snacks. Everyone on the van went in at once so it was easy to shoplift some candy. One of the older girls on the bus liked to tease me. "Hey, Brooke, I dare you to get a *Playboy* magazine," she joked. I would have to shoplift it because I was not old enough to buy it. If I had asked my mom for candy money, she would have given it to me, but shoplifting was more fun. I grabbed two Crunch bars for Holly and me and then grabbed the *Playboy* magazine. I had always wondered what was in *Playboy*, and the older girls would think I was cool for stealing it. Holly and I got back on the van into my usual area in the back corner, and I busted out the Crunch bars. Then we started looking at the *Playboy*. It was kind of cool to see all those naked women, and it excited me. One of the older girls grabbed the magazine from me. I didn't get the *Playboy* back until I was about to get off of the van. I bent down to tie my shoe and dropped the *Playboy* down the sewer hole. I hoped my mom wasn't watching. I kind of liked *Playboy*, and I planned on getting another one as soon as possible. Maybe I would get one to keep in my room.

Holly and I decided to go to the mall to buy a present for Lee's birthday party, which was in two weekends. It was a sleepover party. I probably would go and not sleep over because I was always afraid *they* would find me during the night, and I wouldn't be able to get help. I tried to do everything possible to stay in safe situations. Plus, I couldn't sleep over at people's houses unless I brought the Pepto with me.

I was allowed to be in the mall without my mom for two hours, so we shopped for two hours. My mom only drove us to the mall after she had made a thorough examination of the cut on my arm to make sure I didn't need to go to the doctor. She poked and prodded the cut and almost made it bleed again. My mom looked up my records, and fortunately I had just had a tetanus shot. When she asked what had happened, I told her about a sharp nail hanging out of the doorway in the little house. She tried to call the school to tell them about the nail, but I told her that I already pulled it out and threw it away. She suspected nothing. I was safe to go the mall. She wrapped my arm all up again, and we rode in the backseat of the gold Volvo station wagon.

Holly wanted to look at the music store, and I wanted to look in the jewelry store. We went to both and many other stores in the mall. Eventually, we found the perfect gift, a Dick Tracy movie and a turtle stuffed animal. At 5:00 p.m we got in the car, and my mom drove Holly home. Holly kept the presents for Lee's party because I told her I wasn't sure if I was going. I walked her to the door and said hello to her mom and her two parrots. "Hello, hello," the parrots responded. On the ride home I tried to pretend I was sleeping, but my mom wanted to talk.

She wanted to hear about my recent homework assignments, books I was reading, people I talked to, and most importantly, how I was feeling. I spent the whole ride talking with as much animation as I could muster up about the "choose your own adventure" book I was reading. I told her about the characters and every twist and turn they took depending on which action I chose. Finally we got home, and I headed for my room. I told my mom I wanted to talk on the phone in private before dinner.

I took the phone with me, but I couldn't decide who to call. I felt bad, very bad. There was no good word to describe my feelings. I wanted to talk to someone, but I was too afraid. I wanted to cry, but I didn't know how. I felt like doing everything and nothing, all at the same time. I called my friend Dara and asked her if she and Shelby wanted to play. Ten minutes later Dara and her sister Shelby rang the doorbell. We played Nintendo. Sometimes when I focused on something, *they* stopped talking to me, but not this time. *They* were yelling at me while I played Nintendo. *"You should die. You do not deserve a life. You are such a bad child. Watch out tonight we are going to kill you,"* the voices screamed. I just sat there and stared at the Nintendo screen. I was the master of Tetris. I could get 150 lines.

"Dinner!" called my brother. Dara and Shelby walked home, and I sat down for dinner with my brothers. My parents were going out to eat. I loved my dad, and I wished that he wasn't going out; I rarely got to see him because he worked so much. When I did get to see him, I felt protected by him even though he didn't intend on protecting me. I spent the weekend writing in my journal, playing soccer, and lying on my bed, waiting for death. Monday morning came around again faster than I would have liked, and I waited at the window for the van to come. Home made me feel safer than school, but I had to endure.

When I got to school five minutes before the bell, there was a big commotion around the lockers. Seven girls had written a note about how they hated Ann and how she was such a bitch and a slut. The girls were excited that they had written and organized a note about Ann, but they were too afraid to put it in her locker. Since they didn't want to throw it away, I told them I'd take care of it. I didn't sign it, but I took it outside and buried it in the sandbox. I figured no one would find it, but we would always know where it was.

One of the girls who signed the note told Ann what she'd done because she felt guilty, and Ann dug up the note. Even though I hadn't signed it, Ann was mad at me for burying it. She said I'd made the girls write it, and she told the teacher. I didn't care too much. As long as my parents didn't find out, I didn't care what trouble I got into. The teacher sent me to talk to the counselor, and she made all the other girls make up and apologize.

This wasn't my first time in the counselor's office. I often got in trouble for being disrespectful. The counselor thought only a person with low self-esteem acted out. I didn't have low self-esteem, I just was sometimes bored in class and disagreed with what the teacher said. Anyway, the counselor started off by reprimanding me. I told her that all I did was bury the note, and I promised that I wasn't lying. She believed me but took advantage of my being in her office to ask me some questions.

"How do you feel about your parents? Do they ever hurt you?"

"No," I replied

"And what about your brothers? Do they put too much pressure on you?"

"No," I replied again. "Let's just get through this crap. No one hurts me, no one touches me, no one makes me feel bad. Any other questions or can I get back to class?"

"Fine, Brooke, and if you ever need any help you just knock on my door."

"Okay, I will." I stood up to leave. I wanted to tell her that I felt scared, that I was going to be killed, but I thought she was one of *them*. I thought she was just being nice to get me to open up so she could beat me and then kill me. But I stayed strong.

I heard her following me as I left her office, but when I turned around, there was no one there. I sat down at my desk and opened my journal. The topic on the board said: the most embarrassing moment of your life. I looked around and tried to make eye contact with my friends, but they all seemed mad at me. It was as if they had all convinced themselves that I had made them write the note and get into trouble. I figured, "They'll get over it." I turned to my journal, but I could not think of anything to write.

I kept such careful tabs on myself because I was afraid of getting caught that I never lose my inhibitions enough to be embarrassed. Finally I jotted down a quick story about my dad yelling at me in public, and I closed my journal. If only I could write to my teachers in my journal about my real thoughts.

During gym, we went up to the ice-skating rink. I loved skating and was out on the rink while everyone was still putting their skates on. I had hockey skates like the boys because they were more comfortable. I kind of wished I had gotten in trouble, and someone would have thought that something was wrong with me. If only I could figure out a way to make someone realize I was in danger without actually telling them, I could get help. But there was no help out there for me, I was a terrible person, and I should die, or at least that's what *they* thought.

CHAPTER 2

Anonymous Notes

They were still bothering me when I started middle school in fifth grade. I got my own locker, my own gym uniform, my own Trapper Keeper (a notebook), but I still felt like I didn't have my own friends. Sure, there were people I liked to hang out with, but they didn't know the "real" me. Nobody did. I blamed myself mostly for not having friends because I was so busy lying and acting how I thought a fifth grader should act; I just had my friends as part of my image. Every time someone asked me a question, I had to think twice before answering to make sure I said the right thing. "Brooke, do you have any gum?" a friend asked. I had to think it through. *Should I have gum? Will she think I'm weird if I have a gum? Will I have the right kind of gum?* My safest bet was to say, "No, sorry I don't have any gum." This way I didn't risk being able to give gum to her but not my other friends. I also don't risk her not liking my kind of gum and thinking I'm weird. Every little thing was a big thing to me.

Anyone in my class would say I was popular and nice. I didn't have a best friend, but I had lots of people I played with and hung out with. To everyone, I was social and happy. No one knew the truth that I was hearing voices telling me to hurt myself and other people. The voices didn't want me to be happy; *they* wanted me to die. *They* said, *"Die, die, die. You're going to die. We're going to kill you. The first time you slip or mess up, your life will be taken"*

Sometimes I didn't know what *they* wanted me to do or not

do. I had to do everything perfectly. It was hard work ignoring *them* and making *them* invisible to everyone else. I had a method of reading a series of books and finding the best qualities of all the characters and forming a personality for myself that way. I wanted to be as smart as Pippi Longstocking, as brave as Anne Frank, and as nice as the girls in *The Baby-Sitters Club*. I did a pretty good job of making a person for me to be by putting together parts.

No one questioned my health, physical or mental. I basically had two lives. I had the life that everyone saw, where I was a ten-year-old girl who was smart, athletic, and nice. Then there was the part of me that nobody saw, where I shut my window shades to keep out bad people, and I sat watching a blank TV because to me it was not blank, I saw people on it. I also had dreams of becoming a serial killer. I read everything I could find about serial killers. I wanted the death penalty though, and they didn't give that to children in any state.

I had an advisor in fifth grade who came closest to knowing what was going on. Her name was Mrs. Whick, and in addition to being my advisor, she was the headmaster of the middle school. She was a big black woman. Her curls flew out in every direction, and she usually wore loose long skirts and blouses. I always knew she was coming because I could hear her heals clicking on the tiled floors of the hallways. I loved her. Not romantic love, but a friendly/admiring kind of love. The other teachers told her that I was a disruption, but she didn't kick me out because she knew that I didn't have "real" behavior problems. I don't think she knew about the voices or the people trying to kill me, but she might have. Sometimes when I lay in bed at night I imagined conversations I had with Mrs. Whick. I imagined telling her about *them* and her understanding and making it all better. In real life though I was never able to tell anyone.

One day my science teacher lost my test paper and asked me if I would mind retaking it. "Please, Brooke," she begged, "I will give you the exact same exam that you took yesterday. There is no way for me to grade you unless you take the exam again."

"There is no way I am going to retake a test to accommodate for your disorganized mess," I answered. "You should take a lesson from me on how to be organized instead of making me take the test again."

I had a big mouth for an eleven-year-old. I got kicked out of class for being disrespectful and sent to Mrs. Whick's office. Mrs. Whick told me something that I will never forget. "Even if you are right, making the other person feel stupid only gets you into trouble. Keep your comments to yourself unless they are respectful." I didn't adhere to this new policy right away, but I kept it in mind. About halfway through high school, I finally learned how to follow Mrs. Whick's advice.

Middle school was grades five through eight. As I got older I couldn't resist trouble. One time in sixth grade the voices told me to light a telephone booth on fire, so I did. I was scared of the voices, and I thought *they* would kill me if I didn't comply. It was midwinter, and we were ice-skating around the rink during PE. I went into the hockey booth to tie my skates tighter, and I found a red Bic lighter. *"Fire, fire, fire. Light the rink on fire. Light the rink on fire,"* the voices chanted. Instead I went outside, and when I saw the telephone booth, I decided to set it on fire. Some of my friends followed me outside. Four of us took turns lighting the phone book. We couldn't light anything else because nothing would light. After about five minutes I knew we would get caught if we waited any longer so we rushed back into the gym. We didn't make a pact, but we all knew that none of us would tell on anyone. I should have thought twice about trusting my friends because I always end up being the one blamed when a group of kids gets into trouble. Fortunately, my friends kept quiet. They knew that they would get in just as much trouble as I even though I was the ring leader and they were the followers.

When PE was over, we walked back down the hill, and we could see the phone book still on fire, and there were ashes going everywhere. It looked like other parts of the phone booth were starting to catch fire. The teachers waited up at the rink for the next grade to come so they didn't see the burning phone booth until I was long gone. I went home that night, and I was such a hard-core, practiced liar that no one even noticed that I did anything. I did not feel bad about what I had done; I just went on with my life. In homeroom the next morning there was an announcement that if anyone had any information about the phone booth burning down, they should come to the office at any time. Mrs. Whick came into every homeroom class and gave a lecture about desecrating school property and how fire is dangerous and we could have started a big fire. While Mrs. Whick was talking I made eye contact and acted disturbed by the whole thing so she wouldn't have a clue that I was a part of the fire-setting. Even though I loved Mrs. Whick, I didn't trust her completely. I never turned myself in, and none of my friends did either.

Also in sixth grade was when some of the kids in my class started to go behind the school by the fence and smoke. I liked to hang out with them, but I didn't actually like to smoke. It tasted nasty, and I heard it would make it harder for me to breathe when I played soccer. Soccer was my life. I played on a select team, and even though I wasn't great, I was good enough to be on a traveling team. We traveled all over Pennsylvania for tournaments and games. In the winter I played indoors. When I was playing soccer, I felt safe and distracted. It was a temporary break from life, even more so than Nintendo.

I went through a lot of physical changes that almost made me quit soccer, which could have been disastrous. I got glasses. I could not play with them, but I needed them to see the ball. I solved this problem by getting contact lenses. I was young for contact lenses, but I was a clean, careful person so the doctor said it was okay. The second big physical change was that I got my period. I didn't tell anyone for four months. I just stole the supplies I needed from the grocery store when I went for bike rides.

I pulled my bike up to the bike rack outside of the ThriftWay, and I took my backpack into the store with me. The cameras were in aisles 1, 3, 5, 7, and 8, the vegetable aisle. I knew where the cameras were because I had a baby-sitter who worked at ThriftWay, and I asked her to find out for me, and she did. I shoplifted frequently and never got caught, so I think the baby-sitter gave me good information. The women's products were in aisle 3, between the shampoos and the diapers. I grabbed a box of pads that would fit in my bag, and I carried it over to the paper goods aisle where there were no cameras. Just as I was shoving it in my bag someone who worked in the store walked by. I acted like nothing was going on, and the employee did not even look twice at me. Mission successful.

But soon, it became a problem when I was playing soccer. I was only ten years old, so I had no friends to turn to about women's issues. I didn't want to tell my mom because I knew she would think it meant I was becoming a woman, when in reality, I felt like I was becoming more of a man. I wanted to be a male desperately, but my developed body and then my period kept getting in the way. I played with the boys at recess and gym, I dressed like a boy, I even studied how my brothers talked so I could talk like a boy. I thought that I was born with the wrong sex, and the only thing I could do was keep acting like a boy and hope that I could eventually figure out a way to change myself. I was eleven when my aunt got married I wanted to wear a suit instead of a dress, but I was not allowed. I was embarrassed by my girl parts so I never wore anything where people could see my underwear lines. I was also concerned that people could see into my shirt so I couldn't wear the circle neck shirts from Gap that everyone my age was into.

Eventually I told my mom about my period. She taught me how to use feminine products so I could still play soccer without thinking about it. That was a relief.

In sixth grade I got in trouble for a lot of things that I didn't remember even doing. I was having blackouts where I would blink once, and hours of time would have gone by. One time I kissed a boy without even knowing about it until I heard about it the next day from a girl who so kindly told me that no one could believe that I'd kissed him. I hated losing time. It made me feel like I was just super forgetful. One time I was in class, and I blinked, and all of a sudden I found myself in the office. I had no idea what I did to get to the office. I stood up to walk out, and the secretary said, "Brooke, don't you listen? Mrs. Whick told you to stay put." I sat back down. I had so much anxiety that I'd revealed my secrets and would be killed for it that I started to cry. I never cried. When Mrs. Whick came back to call me into the office, I saw another boy in the office. "Why did you hurt him?" asked Mrs. Whick. I didn't want to let on that I didn't know what had happened so I just apologized profusely and promised it would never happen again. I somehow wiggled my way out of a mess. I got clues from my classmates about what I had done. Apparently John (the boy) put his hand on my shoulder to ask me for a pencil, and I turned around and hit him square in the face. I didn't remember any of it; I was just glad that no one got hurt real bad.

In seventh grade I got into the biggest trouble I'd ever been in. I was twelve years old, and as school got harder, the voices got progressively worse. *"Kill Jamie. Kill Jamie,"* the voices were commanding me. *"Steal the knife from the butcher block, put it in your backpack, and bring it to school. Follow Jamie after school. Ask her to go get a soda with you from behind the gym. When you get there, pull the knife out and stab Jamie in the heart. Don't be a wimp. Stab her until she falls down. And then when she's dead for sure, put the knife back into your bag and go home just like any other day. You must do this."* When the voices commanded me, I felt like I had no choice but to follow *them* For about a month I dreaded going to school each day because I knew that I would see my friends and the voices would yell at me to do it. Finally I decided to write an anonymous note to Jamie, telling her when and where I was going to kill her, so I could act like I was going to follow through to please the voices, but nothing would happen because Jamie would avoid the situation, having read the note.

This started out with just one girl, but pretty soon I was writing notes to all of my friends.

> I am going to kill you at 3:15 after school by your locker. I have a knife to kill you with.

They varied a little bit, but they were all typed anonymously. My plan worked. I didn't have to kill anyone, I could just act like I was going to and the voices would be satisfied. Soon though, all of my friends started to notice a pattern that they were receiving anonymous threat letters in their lockers and backpacks and I wasn't. So I had to start writing notes to myself. That was weird because I knew I wasn't going to kill myself, yet I had to keep the situation working. Everyone was scared, and no one knew why they were going to be killed.

If this happened today with the background of all the school shootings, there would probably be a police investigation. I would probably have gotten caught and sent to jail. But as it stood, no one suspected me because I was acting like their friend and carefully dropping the notes. I started to write more descriptive notes saying things like:

> I hate you. I hate you. I hate you. You are going to die, and I am going to be the one to kill you. I have a knife that will kill you.

I became known as the "hate-note writer," only no one knew it was me. I was scared, but I couldn't stop writing hate notes. I didn't really hate people. I was just trying to help them understand why I had to kill them, and I wanted to prevent anything bad from happening.

I went on writing hate notes/death threats for about two months. The teachers had meetings. Our whole grade had to meet in our advisor groups with the principal to figure out if anyone had any clue who was writing the notes. They claimed, "The person is very sick, we just want to help them." I could not give myself up even though I wanted help. I pretended to cry like all the other girls. Then I started writing notes to my teachers. I would write a note and then drop it on the floor of the classroom by someone else's desk. The notes to the teachers were longer, and they said things like:

> I need help, and you are the only one who can help me. I am the author of the hate notes, and I am going to kill somebody if you don't help me. You are a terrible teacher if you can't even figure out which one of your students needs help. I hate you.

I sometimes went on for a whole page about how bad the teachers were. One day I was typing a note on the computer, and I left it for a moment to answer the phone. My dad walked into the computer room and saw the note on the computer. Having gotten numerous letters sent home about hate notes, he knew exactly what it was, and he knew that I was behind the whole thing. My dad approached me. "What are you writing, my dear?" my dad asked. I was caught. I immediately lied and said, "I wrote them, but I didn't mean it, and I don't know why I did it." He said maybe I was bored in school, and I was reaching out for attention. I agreed, even though I knew that was not the cause.

When my mom got home, they made me call the principal and all the teachers to whom I had written notes. I had never called a teacher at home before. "Hello, this is Brooke Katz."

"Hello, Brooke, how can I help you? Is everything all right?" my history teacher asked.

"I am the hate-note writer. I'm really sorry." I felt stuck because I couldn't give up the voices and tell my teacher the true reason for the note writing.

"Why, Brooke? What made you write those notes? Do you really hate people?"

"No," I answered. "I don't really hate anyone. I don't know why I wrote them. I'm sorry, I don't know why."

"Well, we're going to have to have a meeting about this, and

I will talk to the other teachers and administrators." My history teacher had received some of the meanest notes, and I was afraid that they would get me into big trouble. But, she seemed nice over the phone. Maybe she really wasn't too mad.

I called my English teacher and the headmaster of the school too. It was around 8:00 at night, and they were all home. They all wanted to know *why*.

"Hello?" my English teacher asked.

"Hi, this is Brooke Katz. I need to tell you that I am the hate-note writer."

"Brooke, if this is a joke, it's not funny." My teacher didn't even believe that I was really confessing.

"This is not a joke, I really did it. I'm sorry."

"Okay, Brooke, can you tell me why you wrote the hate notes? Do you really hate people?"

I couldn't tell any of them why I did it.

They told me that they would get me some help and that I didn't need to be in so much pain. They told me that they understood how hard middle school can be. I thought, *They have no idea. I wish I could be dealing with the everyday stress of middle school.* Still, I wasn't sure how I was going to get through this. The principal set up a meeting with me and my parents and the two main teachers who were involved (my history and English teachers). I thought I was going to get expelled.

A couple afternoons later I sat in the principal's office with my parents. I wished Mrs. Whick was still the headmaster; she would understand, but she retired after my sixth-grade year. Now I was in seventh grade. I couldn't stop crying. The voices were loud, screaming that I can't trust anyone. *They* thought I was going to give *them* up. But I knew I couldn't tell anyone about the voices. Not only would they not believe me, but if they did believe me, they would probably send me away someplace (I wasn't sure where). I wouldn't get to see my family or friends. I didn't want to be identified as the girl who hears voices. Plus, I was not even sure what *they* were. I thought maybe everyone heard voices, and mine were just being mean.

I sat in the meeting as the principal pulled out every letter that I had written to a teacher, and I had to fess up to every one of them. My parents were in shock, but my dad did say that the letters were well done. They asked me why I had done it, and I said, "I DON'T KNOW!" I told them a million times that I didn't know, but they thought I had a hidden motive. They asked me to leave the room and had one of the teachers leave with me to supervise me. They told my parents that as a consequence I would have to see a psychiatrist and get an evaluation.

I was invited back into the meeting, and the assistant principal said, "Brooke, we will decide your punishment after we hear from the psychiatrist whom you will be seeing." I gulped. I hated doctors, especially ones who ask probing questions. This left me wondering if they were considering kicking me out of school, or if they were going to give me a lenient punishment if I had a mental illness.

I went home with my parents, and they told me that they would be picking me up directly from school the next day, and I would be going to see a psychiatrist. We told my brothers that I had gotten in trouble at school and that we were going to a meeting. I was twelve so they took me to a child psychiatrist whom the school had recommended. I told my parents that I would go, but I would refuse to talk about the notes. If she brought up the notes, I would stop talking.

I told the shrink that I would talk about anything except the notes. When my parents left the room, the first question the doctor asked was, "So, Brooke, why did you write those notes?" I told her to screw herself, and I got angry and refused to answer any of her questions.

The psychiatrist talked to my parents without me. I don't know what she said, but I never had to go back to that shrink or any other until I chose to much later. In the meeting that followed with the assistant principal, she said that I did not have to tell my peers that I was the note writer, but she suggested that I tell my friends. The school year was almost over, and I knew I was moving to Seattle with my family at the end of the school year, so I decided to tell my friends and let them choose whether the news spread or not.

I told them individually, with my closest friend Rachel last. Rachel was the most angry because, like the others, she didn't understand. If I didn't hate her, why did I write hate notes and give them to her? And if I didn't hate myself, why did I give hate notes to myself? I wished so much that I could tell her about the voices and my desires to kill people, but I was too scared. I was confused myself. Before the school year ended I went to the middle school guidance counselor. I made an appointment, I showed up, but I couldn't say anything. I just sat there and cried. The counselor said, "If you're not going to talk I can't help you. You can't be helped unless you're ready to do some work." That made me angry because I was doing some work. I was working all day every day, trying not to listen to the voices, trying to keep myself and everyone else safe. That man made me never want to talk to a school counselor ever again. He made me think that they are all stuck-up, self-righteous people. Although in high school, I did find a school counselor who helped me more than anyone. She was anything but stuck up and self-righteous.

So school didn't end on a happy note. My friends "forgot" about the notes and threw a going-away party for me. We slept over at one girl's house and sang and painted tattoos on each other. I told everyone that I would write, but to this day I only have kept in contact with one middle school friend and that is because our families are close.

That summer before I moved to Seattle I was lonely. I had moved away from my old friends, but I hadn't made any new friends yet. I had all sorts of ideas of how I was going to move across the country and leave everything behind. I wanted to be trouble free. I wanted to be happy, free from *them*. Later, when I still couldn't get rid of the voices, I realized that my troubles were a part of *me*, and I could not just choose to leave them behind.

My family spent the summer being "homeless." We traveled around Europe with the whole family. France had the best cheese. My grandfather lives in France so we stayed at his house. In August, we moved into our house in Mercer Island, Washington. Over the summer the voices had pretty much left me alone. In my first night in the new house, though, *they* came in the open window. *"We found you, you bitch; you can't run away from us."* I rolled over in my new bed, devastated that *they* had followed me. I made a promise in my journal that I wouldn't let *them* take over my life.

I had no friends so I signed up for the recreational soccer team, hoping to meet some people. Even though I hadn't been playing all summer, I was good enough to be on the club team, but the tryouts for the club weren't until the fall.

The recreational team was where I met Britney, my future best friend. Britney and I went shopping before school started, and my wardrobe completely changed. My pants got baggier, and my shirts got bigger, I wanted to be grunge. I bought a hat that I wore every day of the eighth grade. I wore it backward, and I tied my hair up underneath it. Britney was tall and thin, and I was about average height and average size. We couldn't fit into each other's clothes unfortunately.

One day we took my little brother, Phil, shopping for school clothes. We picked out a whole wardrobe of little punk clothes, and my mom let us buy about half of it.

My only other friend was our housekeeper, Lisa. She would talk to me about how nervous I was, what classes I was taking, and how I was going to meet all the cute guys. She didn't know that more important to me than making new friends was getting rid of *them*. She stayed with us for the whole time I lived in Seattle, and she got to be a good friend. Britney and I hung out and spent a lot of time at the beach. After all, we lived on an island; there was lots of water around. Groveland Beach became our late-night home. We would go there after the lifeguard left, and we would jump off the docks. I also met other friends through Britney. My parents were so happy that I was doing well and making friends that they were more lenient than I would have expected. They normally would not have let me go swimming in the dark.

CHAPTER 3

I Love to Sing

"Yes, sir, I did it," I answered Dr. Hatch, the principal of my new school, Islander Middle School. "I inserted swear words in the choir song during our rehearsal," I confessed. "But you don't know the whole story," I argued.

"Tell me the rest of the story, Brooke."

"It started on the first day of class. The teacher, Mr. Cane, hated me. I was with two people whom I had met, and I wanted to sit by them, but Mr. Cane told me that I was going to be a soprano and my new friends were altos. I was upset because he never had even heard me sing but obviously just wanted me away from my friends. I took my seat with all the other sopranos. We started singing notes, and I knew I couldn't sing at all, and I would make everyone around me sound worse, so I kept my mouth shut. Weeks passed, and I never sang. We had a concert, and I just stood there with my mouth shut. People noticed, and word got back to Mr. Cane that I didn't sing.

"'Today,' he said, 'we're going to sing solos, and Brooke is going to be first.' Of course I refused. I got so frustrated that I almost cried in front of the whole class. Finally he gave up on me singing a solo and turned on the music for the whole class to sing. I was furious because I had been humiliated. I don't know why he just didn't leave me alone. I sang out loud swear words, and I guess I sang louder than I thought because everyone laughed except for Mr. Cane. He sent me to see you. He said if I'd rather be somewhere else then I could sit in the office and never come to choir again. So that's how I ended up here. I know I shouldn't have done it, but he shouldn't have embarrassed me either."

"Well, Brooke, you can't just act out when you feel like you have been treated unjustly. In the future I want you to come to me, and I will help you sort out the situation before you get in trouble. For now, you will sit in the office until I talk to the other administrators and find something for you to do during this period. There's a red chair in the attendance office that you can sit in. Goodbye." That red chair became my private throne. I sat there every time I got kicked out of class. It became a comfort seat; whenever I felt unsure of where I was or where I was going I was able to find the red chair, and I just sat there until I felt calm again. No one talked to me while I was sitting in the red chair because they thought I was being punished. The attendance lady told me that I could sit there all day if I pleased.

Mr. Hatch had let me off the hook. He would probably call my parents, but he didn't mention it, and I didn't want to remind him. I would also probably get a referral which means I would go to detention. I sat in the red chair, and when the bell rang, Mr. Hatch came to find me to excuse me to my next class. He said that he had put me on *level 3* which means I would go to detention for two weeks, and if I got in trouble again, I would move to *level 4,* which has a lot of restrictions. He also told me that he called my parents. He didn't say how they reacted, but I assumed it would not be too pleasant for me when I got home.

My parents were angry at me for being disrespectful, but I apologized and said it wouldn't happen again. Not only was I pleased to be able to start my new identity in Seattle, but my parents were overall happy too. Little did I know that after Dr. Hatch sent me to the red chair in the attendance office, the red chair would become my seat for two hours a day most days. Also, my visits with the administrators became more and more frequent.

After that day, when I got in trouble in choir, I started getting yellow slips during class. A *yellow slip* is a little piece of paper that the office TAs (teacher assistants) deliver to teachers, and the teachers hand them out to the named student. The yellow slip either says to see the counselor, vice principal, the principal, or the psychologist. They usually specify: at once, when you have a chance, or at the end of the period. I was receiving about three yellow slips a day. I was afraid to go to the office though because I thought that if I got trapped in a room with a counselor (where I was usually going), she would ask me a million questions, and I would break down and tell her about the voices.

The voices were still there, but *they* weren't getting me in as much trouble as *they* did before we moved. Still, *they* ruled my life. *They* were behind most bad decisions that I was making. It was easy to hide *them* from my friends and teachers. I was acting like such a punk anyway that people just thought that I was acting out for attention. *They* told me who to talk to, who was safe, and what to do. I didn't realize until much later that *they* were lying to me, tricking me, and getting me into trouble. Back to the yellow slips, whenever I got one I would just throw it away. Most students liked getting yellow slips, but I hated it. It was so embarrassing for the whole class to watch me get handed a slip which meant the whole class knew I was in trouble.

I stayed on *level 3* for months just for getting in trouble doing little things like talking out, or being excessively late to class. The voices would hold me up, telling me to go places to find things. And then when someone asked me where I was going, I had to lie because I couldn't give away the voices' secret spots. There was never anything hidden, but I faithfully followed the voices anyway for fear of *them* killing me.

One thing that helped me stay focused on life and not drift into my own world was soccer. I played on a rec team with about fifteen other girls from my school. I met my best friends on that team. Britney was one of the best ones on the team, and she was nice to me so we just hit it off. I became friends with her and her group of friends instantly. Soccer was three times a week, and I always saw Britney there. We also started hanging out together outside of school sometimes. Britney was clean and clear of most trouble, but I still remained constantly in trouble. We tried to help each other—I tried to make her a little more outgoing, and she tried to help me be more insightful. We made a perfect match, and she was my best friend.

One day we were at our friend Rachel's house, and we were playing with her Nintendo. Rachel had lots of animals, and they were annoying. Her cat stood on my head and scratched me. I stood up in a fit of anger and threw the cat across the room. It came back, and just when it was about to scratch me again, I put it in the microwave. I cooked it for two seconds in a Fisher Price microwave. No one helped me cook the cat. Rachel just watched and laughed. The cat ran away, and I never saw it again. Rachel moved to Arizona soon after, and I never heard if her mom found the stupid cat. I hated cats.

Every morning I rode the bus to school, and every afternoon I rode the late bus home after detention. Detention was tedious. I had to sit in a trailer and not make any noise for an hour. The desks were chairs with an arm that folds up as a desk. They were hard to sit in for a whole hour because they were made of wood. I was allowed to do my homework, but I never had any because school was so easy so I just sat there and thought. The silence brought out the voices, and every now and then I would talk to *them*, and the teacher would yell at me, and I would stop. Detention was boring, and none of my friends were ever in there with me. For the most part, all my friends were well behaved. When I would ride the late bus home, I would get off at the center.

The center was the small downtown Mercer Island area that had two grocery stores, a drugstore, a McDonald's, a video store, and a skateboard park. I would meet my friends, and we would just hang out. When I told my mom that I was hanging out, she thought I was smoking pot so she refused to let me hang out at the center. I disobeyed her and went there anyway. It was fun to be devious. As I was hanging out at the center, I made new friends. Britney remained my friend, but I quickly lost contact with the people who had accepted me when I was new. I started hanging out with high schoolers and sixth graders.

I found friends who were into burning themselves. They did it with cigarettes or burning paper clips or hangers. I told them about my cutting, and we had big self-mutilation parties at one girl's apartment. I felt so good to be around people who approved of me for who I was. Some of the older people with whom I was hanging out were into drugs. At that point I wanted to try anything to make me feel better. I was feeling so depressed and confused all the time. As the year went on, the voices were getting louder, and I was seeing things more than I ever had before. The giant men were following me and appearing in every window that was not covered. The TV was like a screen that showed people shooting at me even when my mom was watching the news. I could also hear noises coming from the TV. Sometimes I saw images of dead people just floating around in the air. When I got too close to them they screamed at me even though they were dead.

I tried smoking marijuana. Looking back, it made me paranoid. At the time I did not know what paranoid was. I ran in circles because I thought people were following me. I screamed that I didn't want to let *them* kill me. The people I was with took the marijuana away from me. I tried it once more, but nothing happened. I decided that marijuana was not the drug for me. I took speed. I snorted crystal methamphetamine. That became my drug of choice. I don't think I was ever addicted, but I loved the stuff. I knew that it was addicting so I only used it on special occasions. That worked for me. No one knew that I was using drugs. No one really understood me at all. I was a good student academically, and I got straight A's based on my work, but my behavior was terrible, and I was constantly acting out. I was disrespectful and hyper. The teachers could not deal with me. They found a few solutions to help me. One thing that did help was to give me an assignment and then place my desk in the corner facing the wall. This way my mind would be busy doing work, and I had no distractions beside the voices. One other solution that the teachers used was to give me harder work than they gave to the rest of the class. This solution made it so I couldn't complain of boredom and blame my acting out on being bored. I was never sent to a "resource room" or anything like that, and I don't think that would have helped because academically I was fine. I aced most of my tests in every subject.

In journalism class, they split us up so that half of us went to a therapy group with the drug and alcohol counselor every day instead of going to journalism class. We got to talk about our feelings, and the other group got to make a newspaper. I found this very unfair so I constantly complained and refused to participate. This made them think I was hiding something. I started getting even more yellow slips. I still threw them away and never went. At this point I was getting phone calls home every day from my English and history teachers. I told my parents stories about how crazy my teachers were and how stupid they were. I let them think that the teachers were picking on me. This way when the teachers called our house, my parents didn't want to talk to them. If they did talk, my parents were angry with the teachers, not me. My parents believed me that I was getting picked on because I would just tell them half of the story. I would tell how I got kicked out of chorus, and I would tell about how the teacher made me sit with the sopranos. I never had any homework, and my progress reports all had straight A's. My parents never punished me when the teachers called home, we just had discussions. There was no reason to believe that anything was wrong because I was showing no red flags or warning signs. I spent most of my time at home with the radio blasting in my room. I had friends, I ate well, I was a little rude, but my parents thought every young girl was a little rude to her parents and teachers.

One day the guidance counselor came into my classroom and found me. She took me back to her office. We sat, and I told her that I was not acting out, I was just acting like myself, and I was bored in school. She questioned me about my friends, asking who used drugs. I told her that I don't know anyone who uses drugs. I hid all my cut marks from her because I knew I could get in big trouble from that. She told me that it appeared as though

I was having trouble adjusting, and I should feel free to talk to her whenever I wanted to.

I left her office and went out behind the school. I considered climbing onto the roof but decided that it wasn't worth the risk of getting caught. One talk with the counselor in a day is enough. I sat down on the ground, and I cried. I hadn't cried for several years, and I didn't know how to stop it. I cried because I was scared that I was going back to being what I was like before I moved to Seattle, and I didn't want to be like that. I cried because the voices were following me everywhere and putting too much pressure on me. I cried because although I liked my independence, I missed my mom and dad. I thought about running away from home, but then I decided that was a temporary solution to a permanent problem. I thought about killing myself, but I would cause too much pain to Britney. I just sat and cried.

The lunch bell rang, and kids started coming. I decided to go back to the counselor's office. I knew I was in trouble, and I didn't know her very well, but she was my only hope. The door was open, but I knocked anyway. She called out, "Just one minute," and then she looked up at me and instantly hung up the phone. She was glad to see me. She shut the door and closed the blinds. I just sat there. I kept seeing her face transform, and I don't know if she was making faces or if it just looked that way to me. The voices were screaming at me not to talk. She asked me questions. I did not respond. She touched my leg, and I withdrew. I don't remember what she said, but I blinked, and all of a sudden I was at my house and three hours had passed. I felt fine and couldn't remember much of the day except when I talked to the guidance counselor. I was proud of myself for not breaking down completely.

I went to bed early, and I woke up early as usual. I had to be at class at 7:10 at the high school (I had math with the ninth graders). I woke up at around 4:00, and I waited for the alarm to go off. I didn't want anyone in my house to know that I was awake. Sometimes I woke up early, other times I slept through the alarm. I felt refreshed, and I went to geometry. In geometry I sat in the back with my two friends, Carol and Leroy. Carol was my math buddy, and she was in my math class until she graduated from high school. We worked well together, and Carol helped keep me focused on math. Because I had math at the high school, I had an open period during the day at middle school (actually I had two open periods because I had choir open). During the choir period I sat in the red chair and read. During the math open period I tutored a seventh-grade boy, Ray, who was failing. He was a curly-haired skater. The first thing I did with him was organize his binder. Then I helped him with all his subjects, especially math. Within a month we improved his grades to Bs and Cs which was a big improvement from all Ds and Fs. One day Ray got out his skateboard, and we took a break from studying, and he taught me how to do a kickflip. He let me borrow his board to practice for five minutes every day, and eventually I got it.

One day Ray's history teacher saw us practicing with the skateboard, and she flipped out. "A tutor is supposed to be responsible. You are teaching this boy bad study habits. Get over here, I have a punishment suited for you two." She made us crawl on our hands and knees, picking up scraps of paper from the floor outside her room. If I took a break, she dumped more paper on the floor. After about thirty minutes, I stood up, told her to screw herself, and left. Ray was afraid that she would give him a bad grade so he stayed. The next day I saw Ray, and we decided to forget the skateboarding tricks for a while. I loved math, and I loved tutoring Ray, therefore everything worked out with me taking geometry at the high school during first period.

One thing that did not improve at the same rate as tutoring was my social skills. I hung out with punks mostly who didn't have anywhere else to fit in. One exception was my eighth-grade boyfriend, Caleb. I don't know how it started, but I had a few friends in eighth grade with me, and most of my friends were in sixth grade. My favorite sixth grader was Caleb. At first, all the girls had a crush on him; Kate, Teresa, and Rachel all wanted to go out with him. Caleb chose me. I was so happy. He was cute, smart, and hilarious. I don't know why he chose me, but I remember the day when he asked me out. We sat together at lunch, hung out during break, and spent every hour we weren't at school or soccer together. Either I went to his house, or he went to my house, or we met at the center.

Caleb was a prankster, and I was too when I was with him. We stole from the drugstore and took the bus from one end of the island to the other and then ran off without paying. I hated being touched, but as the relationship progressed, we started touching more and kissing at every opportune moment. I felt him, and he felt me, but only through clothes. We never did anything more than kissing. I think that I snuck my tongue too far down his throat one time, and then he was hesitant after that. We stopped going out in the spring. He was busy, and so was I; we just didn't have time for a playful relationship anymore.

I liked spending time with Caleb, and I was sad to let him go. The thing was that I was overwhelmed by the touching. It made me feel out of control, and I couldn't stand not being in total control all the time.

The thing that Caleb (or anyone else for that matter) did not know was that I was also seeing other people while I was dating him. Most of the other people I was seeing were girls. I was experimenting with my sexuality and hooking up with all sorts of people. I only remember bits and pieces, but I remember leaving school with girls and going behind the Mercer Island Country Club and making out. I had so much fun. Then I remember having them at my house, and my parents trusted me in my room with girls because they had no idea what I was doing. That experimentation continued on through high school, but I stopped remembering what happened soon after middle school. I was so anxious about touching that I blacked out intense physical relationships.

I used to go to parties on the weekends. These parties usually were just with my middle school friends (sixth—and eighth-grade friends), and there was usually no drinking or drugs. Britney, my best friend, did not know anything about my secrets with dating girls or trying drugs. She knew that I skipped school and acted out, but I was afraid to let her know any more than my parents because she was so close to them that I thought she might crack if questioned.

Well, one night I went to a party at Kate's house, and I don't remember anything else except that I woke up in the middle of the night, on the floor, with no clothes on. There were people sleeping all around me. I felt like I had just been placed down in the middle of a scene. I felt a sharp pain between my legs, and I was bleeding. I had no other injuries. I didn't want to freak out, I figured that I had sex with a guy and my body was used to girls so I was bleeding and sore. I didn't know who the guy was, or what I consented to and what was done against my will. It's hard when I don't remember things. I must have blacked out. I found my clothes and sat outside on the porch staring at the trees. When it got light out I went back inside and watched everyone slowly wake up. I was afraid to go back to sleep. I wanted to go to Planned Parenthood the next day, but I didn't have a car, and my parents said they never wanted to see or hear of me taking the public bus without permission. The restriction on taking the public bus had never stopped me before, but I didn't feel so brave and obnoxious now. I felt more scared and confused. I didn't really want to go, and in my mind, not being able to ride the bus alone justified my not going. I knew if I told them the whole situation my parents would understand, but I felt ashamed and confused that I didn't even know what happened. I didn't tell anyone, not even Britney.

At this point I realized that I probably needed some help because I was headed down the wrong path. I went to school Monday morning and knocked on the counselor's door. "Brooke!" she was surprised. "Come on in, I was just thinking about you." I sat down and tried to figure out how I was going to ask for help. I said to her, "What would you do if you had a student who wanted to be good and did well on tests and papers but just couldn't stop acting out?" She said, "I would talk to that student about why they are afraid to reach their full potential, and I would get the parents involved in some family treatment." Then she noticed my clothes. They were the same clothes I was wearing the last time I saw her. They were dirty and smelly, and I wore lots of layers.

"Is someone hurting you, Brooke?" I guess she had to ask that, but it annoyed me. "No," I answered. "And if they were I would deal with it myself. I don't know why I came here. I'm sorry to waste your time, you can't help me."

I slammed the thick wooden door behind me and ran down the blue-carpet sixth-grade hall to the bathroom. I pulled a razor out of my wallet and cut my stomach once. One time was enough for me to see the blood so I could calm down. I sat on the dirty floor and tried to concentrate on something peaceful. I think it was all the sexual behavior that was suddenly making my life more difficult to handle. I had no one to talk to. I wanted to die. I thought of taking that razor and cutting my wrist. I knew exactly how to do it, I read about it in a book at the library. One deep horizontal cut along the purple artery, and I could bleed to death in the bathroom at my middle school. That's not how I wanted to die.

I needed to talk to someone more than I needed to die. I didn't have any friends to talk to because I had so many secrets that they did not know.

I stood up, put the blade away, and went to class. I was only a few minutes late, which was my usual. I wanted to get kicked out of class; I hated history. I sat and threw pieces of paper at my friend across the room. Predictably, the teacher threw me out of the room and told me to go to the office. *Yeah, right, would I go to the office?* I needed a walk. I needed to distress. I needed a break from all the noise in my head. No one understood that I acted out when I needed a break or when I was bored, not when I needed attention. I knew plenty of ways to get attention by doing positive, nondisruptive things. I went for my walk, and I must have looked like a bum. When I entered the QFC (grocery store), a man followed me. He thought I was going to steal. I hadn't showered in a couple days, and I was wearing huge jeans about eight inches below my waist with boxers showing and a dirty gray T-shirt under a flannel that I wore every day. When it was cold out I added a fleece vest, but this day was warm. I also wore a yellow-green-and-blue Brazil hat. I wore it backwards and tied my hair in a ponytail underneath the brim. I looked like a boy, and I loved it.

Some days I purposely tried to make myself look like a boy. For me, as I described earlier, it was more than just wanting to look like a boy, I wanted to be one. I wanted to be able to act out more without getting in trouble. I wanted to be able to fight, which I did sometimes but all the girls I fought with were so weak that it was too easy. I wanted the expectation that I would be smart, just because I was a boy. I wanted the expectation and the standards that I would have if I was a boy. Plus, I felt like a boy. I was a boy trapped in a girl's body. There was no way out so I just did the best job I could do pretending to be a boy. In the mirror I thought I looked masculine, and many other people mistook me for a boy. It wasn't a game; it was an activity of everyday life.

The voices were getting worse during my eighth-grade year. *They* started talking more about hurting people. I thought I was done with that. Then *they* started talking about burning things down. During my lunch break I borrowed my friend's lighter and went out by the track to where there were piles of wood because they were doing construction on the school. I lit some paper on fire and stuck it in the cracks of the pile of wood. I thought the whole pile would light, but that never happened. I went back to the lunch room to watch, and nothing really happened. The paper eventually just blew away as a little fireball, and a fire never started. After I did that I realized that I could have just done something huge. My heart raced, and I felt kind of powerful. I could have just set the school on fire.

CHAPTER 4

How Teachers Make a Difference

I sat in my Honors American History class and stared at the TV screen in the front of the room which was showing *The Great Gatsby*. *"Die, die, die, die,"* the voices yelled in my head. It sounded like *they* were coming from outside my head, and I heard *them* in both ears. There were two voices, both male, and both angry. *They* had colors, one was red and the other was blue. Jamie looked at me and made a joke about the character's 1920s attire in the movie. I sort of laughed. I had to be strong. In the past the voices had not been such a strong interruption into my schoolwork. The movie seemed to get louder, and the voices in my head blended with the TV voices. I had to get out of there. I went over to Mrs. Caper and told her I was going to the bathroom. "Will you be coming back?" she asked.

"No," I managed. Mrs. Caper followed me out of the classroom, and I felt the eyes of my fifty classmates staring at me. We sat down on the steps and tears spilled over the edges of my eyes. I felt comfortable with Mrs. Caper. Over the past two months I had spent many hours in her office soliciting help, but without really telling her what I needed help for. She would listen and encourage me to write about my feelings. On the steps that day during American History, Mrs. Caper asked me if I would consider speaking to Mrs. Kreme, the counselor. Mrs. Caper, Mrs. Linne, and Mrs. Kreme were worried about me.

I headed to Mrs. Kreme's office, hoping somehow that she would say I was fine and I would feel better, but I knew that was unrealistic. The whole fall I had been overly active, what I now know is manic. I was playing on three soccer teams, coaching a ten-year-old girls' soccer team, getting A's in my five honors classes, experimenting with my sexuality and having what I judge now to be too much sex, spending time with my family acting like nothing was wrong, and sleeping maybe three hours a night. I was the entertainment at every party, and I couldn't stop talking in class and at home. People thought I was funny and entertaining, and I wasn't even trying. So when Mrs. Caper told me that she wanted me to talk to Mrs. Kreme, I wasn't surprised.

In a way I wanted help. Yet, everyone was so busy, especially Mrs. Kreme. I didn't want to bother anyone. I was not the type to reach out for help, but even though I pretended that I didn't need help, when people noticed that something was wrong, I felt a little bit of relief to go along with my fear that they were figuring out my secret.

Up until the beginning of my junior year I knew nothing about mental illness. When I stopped sleeping, though, I started spending more time reading; I read everything I could get my hands on. This included books like *The Bell Jar* and *An Unquiet Mind*. I began to wonder if I had depression or bipolar disorder. I wondered if I could take medication and feel better. I did not want to go to a therapist though because I was afraid that the voices would kill me. Even though *they* were just voices, *they* had so much power over me.

Mrs. Kreme's door was closed, which meant there was someone in there, but it was the middle of second period so I thought maybe she'd be done soon. I sat down in one of the red cushy chairs and rested my arms on the sides. As I sat there, I was scared—I was scared of Mrs. Kreme finding out about the voices, and I was scared of the voices who were yelling at me. I tried not to cry in case anyone I knew walked by. I was already going to have to explain to my friends why I left history class. About forty minutes later Mrs. Kreme opened her door. People in chairs all around the room stood up. They were all waiting for her. She looked at me and said, "Are you next?" I couldn't answer.

"Okay, come into my office, Brooke." She shut the door behind us.

"I'll just be a minute, Mrs. Kreme, it's just that I'm not feeling too well."

"I can tell that, Brooke. What's wrong?"

The voices were yelling, *"Don't speak Don't tell her. She's mean. She'll kill you. She's got a knife in her drawer"* I stood up and opened the door. Mrs. Kreme jumped out of her seat to prevent me from leaving. "You're not going to get away that easily," she said. I sat down in the chair the furthest away from her. I put my head in my hands, and I cried. Mrs. Kreme tried to touch my back. I jumped. I didn't want anyone touching me. She let me cry for a while, and then she said, "Brooke, I want to help you, but you have to let me." I stood up, wiped the tears off my face, and left. I had done enough work for the day.

When my friends asked, I told them I was bored, and I had gone for a walk during history class. The voices lessened in math class, and I made it through the day without any more crying. I was strong, and I was going to make it through this by myself. I believed that eventually I would work hard enough to earn the life that I deserved. I was such a bad person, but at least I realized why I was being punished. I didn't need any help. When I saw Mrs. Caper in the hall on my way out, she asked how it went with Mrs. Kreme. "She's nice, but I decided I don't need any help." Mrs. Caper frowned, but before she could offer her disapproval, I walked away.

A couple of days later I was in French class, and I got overwhelmed. I sat next to the window, and I saw people—four men—outside the window, trying to come in. *They* were going to kill me. I looked at the door, and there were two more of *them*. I was trapped, and no one else seemed to notice. I packed up my stuff and made a beeline for the door. My teacher, Mrs. Wilder, asked, *"Ca va?"*

"Ca va tres bien," I responded sarcastically, and I headed out the door. If I was going to be killed I wanted it done now, but as I approached the door the men seemed to get out of my way.

Mrs. Wilder followed me into the hallway and told me that I should go to Mrs. Kreme's office. Apparently Mrs. Kreme had warned all my teachers that she was seeing me. I said, "Whatever," and walked out.

The next thing I remember I woke up on Mildred's sofa. I had been sleeping there, and Mildred, a friend, was in the next room doing homework. When I asked, she said I just showed up at her door, and then I fell asleep watching TV. It was 5:00, when I usually went home from the library, so I called my parents. They were so glad to hear from me. Apparently Mrs. Kreme had been calling, as she was concerned that I had missed school, and she didn't know where I was. My parents knew that I skipped class on occasion so they were more confused than worried. Not only had Mrs. Kreme called my home, but she had found my brother and asked him where I was. I was angry because Mrs. Kreme was intruding in my life, and I hadn't invited her in.

The next day at school I immediately went to Mrs. Kreme's office and told her to stay out of my life and never call my parents. "I'm sorry, I was just worried. Where were you?" I told her that I had blacked out and that happened sometimes. I blamed it on my occasional use of methamphetamines. I walked out of her office, got halfway down the hall, and turned around and went back. She was on the phone, but as soon as she got off she shut the door behind me. "Let's try to talk without shutting down," she said. She asked a lot of questions: Was my home safe? Did my parents drink? How did I feel? I tried to be as honest as possible, but I just couldn't tell her about the voices. I told her that I was doing fine, but recently my emotions felt out of control. She asked if I had ever seen a psychiatrist and if I wanted to. I said, "No way."

Mrs. Kreme wanted to see me on a regular basis, twice a week, until I was feeling better. I thought maybe she could help, so despite being told by the voices that she was against me, I tried talking to her. As time passed I lost more and more control of my emotions. I was constantly scared, angry, and confused. I would get confused and overwhelmed, and all I could do was hug my knees to my chest and rock back and forth. I would try to talk, but Mrs. Kreme wouldn't understand me. She said I wasn't making sense. I stopped having so much energy, and I started to feel down.

One day I told Mrs. Kreme about my cutting. I had been cutting myself since I was nine years old, and I got tired of hiding it. I wanted to stop. Surprisingly, she did not freak out, she just told me to be very careful because cutting is very dangerous. She said I needed to see a psychiatrist. I said no immediately, but I contemplated the idea of seeing a doctor.

I had five close friends who were noticing that I was spending so much time with Mrs. Kreme, and they each, individually, asked what was wrong. I told them about the cutting and my confusion and fear, but I didn't tell them about the voices. My friends started talking to Mrs. Kreme on their own. They would tell her they were scared for me, and they would ask questions about what I was going through.

One night I was up cutting myself in my room when two friends stopped by. They came in without knocking and caught me in the act. None of us knew what to do. My parents didn't know so we couldn't tell them. We made a plan. My friends took home all the sharp things in my room that I could use to cut myself. They stayed and talked to me until 2 am. When they got home they told their parents what had happened because they needed an explanation for being home so late on a school night. Their parents promised to keep it a secret as long as I was getting help.

I don't know why, but I didn't want my parents to know anything. That's why I worked so hard to keep up my grades and kept playing soccer even when I felt so bad. I spent at least an hour with Mrs. Kreme every other day. She saw me at my worst, when I was hearing voices and unable to communicate. She encouraged me to tell my parents, but I refused. All my teachers knew something was wrong, but they couldn't figure me out. I did an excellent job of masking my feelings. I became friends with Mrs. Caper and her teaching partner, Ms. Linne, and I spent more than a lot of time after school with them in their office just talking about why I was scared and confused.

Finally one day I decided that I would see a psychiatrist, but I wouldn't tell my parents. I told Mrs. Kreme in the middle of first period, and by the end of the day she had a list of ten names I could call. But first, she suggested I go to the youth and family services counselor (who was free and anonymous) to help figure things out.

I went to the free counselor, and she was a waste of time. She asked me at least twenty times if I was on drugs because she thought that could be the only cause of my behavior. I was clean though so her theory proved wrong. I didn't like her at all, and neither did the voices. *"We will kill you if you tell her anything,"* said the voices. So I told her nothing, except that I would never see her again.

I went home and got out the list of psychiatrists that Mrs. Kreme had given me. I called all ten, and only one was able to see me within a week so I made an appointment. It was hard because they wanted to know my insurance information, but I told them this was a one-time appointment and I would pay in cash. They wanted to know my diagnosis, and I told them I didn't have one. They basically laughed at me. So I had one week before seeing the psychiatrist. I told my friends that I was going to see a psychiatrist, and I finally decided to tell my parents. I went to school and told Mrs. Kreme that I was going to tell my mom, and I asked her to help me. Mrs. Kreme was delighted. This was the day she had been waiting for, the day when I would share my feelings with my parents. This was the only way that I was going to get help. Mrs. Kreme told the principal that she had an emergency and had to miss a meeting. The principal looked at me and nodded as if to say, "Go, help her." She drove me to my house in her blue Acura. My mom was home alone. I walked through the open garage door and took my mom over to the sofa to sit down. My mom sat on the sofa, I sat next to her, and Mrs. Kreme sat on the ottoman.

"Mom," I said, "I'm going to see a psychiatrist. Please don't ask me why . . . I just need to get some help."

"She might need some medication to help with some issues," said Mrs. Kreme.

My mom was shocked. "Is everything okay?" she asked.

"Yes," I lied, everything was far from okay. I was falling apart, and I was trying to reach out for help, but I didn't know how. I asked my mom to tell my dad because I didn't want to answer any questions.

In the car ride back to school I should have felt relieved, but I was so scared. The voices were so loud, and *they* were telling me to kill myself because I had just messed up so bad that I was going to get killed if I didn't kill myself. Mrs. Kreme tried to congratulate me, but I just sat there, mute. I just hoped that I could make it until this psychiatrist appointment and that he could help me.

The night before I was supposed to go to the psychiatrist, I was nervous, scared, and embarrassed. The voices were loud, and I felt like I wanted to die. My dad offered to drive me to my appointment the following day, and I said I would drive myself. "No, I insist," said my dad. Suddenly I started screaming.

"I will only go if I can drive myself. I have been driving for a year, and I know the way," I screamed. My dad yelled back, and we had a screaming fight. This was different than the other fights we'd had because I couldn't calm down. I would make no compromise, and I wanted to cut myself and didn't know what to do. The voices told me to stop talking, so I stopped talking. I just ran around my room in silence. I was freaking out, and my dad joked, "Brooke, you're acting so crazy I think you might need to be in the hospital. If you don't calm down, we're taking you to the hospital." Little did he know that we would end up in the hospital later that night.

My parents gave me thirty minutes to calm down, and I called my friend, Jay. I could trust her. She said it sounded like an emergency, and I should call Mrs. Kreme at home. Normally, I would never call someone for help, especially when they are at home. But, like my friend said, this was an emergency. I called Mrs. Kreme and tried to explain to her that I was hysterical and felt like hurting myself, and I didn't know what to do. "You should go to the ER. Can you get a ride there, or do you want me to come get you?" asked Mrs. Kreme. She was definite. It had been thirty minutes, and my parents came knocking on the door. I put Mrs. Kreme on speaker phone, and she told my parents not to agitate me any more by asking me any questions and to just drive me to the ER at Overlake Hospital and she would meet us there.

My parents were in shock, and I was so scared because the voices were yelling in my head, and I thought *they* were going to kill me. On the way there my dad asked, "Are you sure you want this? Maybe we can work something out?" But I didn't answer. I thought, *I am so messed up that I need to be in the hospital. This is the only way I can be safe.*

Mrs. Kreme met us at the ER, and the first thing they did was give me a sedative to calm me down. The nurse took me by myself and searched me for weapons, then she asked if I wanted my parents or Mrs. Kreme to come back with me. I was afraid of my parents, so I said, "Mrs. Kreme." She's the one whom I trusted. After an hour wait, they gave me a two-hour interview. The social worker asked everything, and when she asked if I heard voices, I said no and kind of laughed. Then the doctor came in and performed a physical exam where he found nothing except the scars from my cutting which he asked me about. By then I had calmed down enough that I asked for my parents to come in. They were so worried and upset it made me feel like I was such a bad child. My mom wanted to know if I had been in a car accident, or if I had been raped. My dad didn't talk much, and he kept leaving to make phone calls.

The psychiatrist came in, and he said that I needed help that they could provide in the Adolescent Partial Day Hospital Program. It was a therapeutic program for kids that lasted from 9 a.m. to 3 p.m. on weekdays. I started crying and told the doctor I couldn't go home. I couldn't tell him that there were people in my room who wanted to kill me or that I was too confused. I just told him that I wanted to be an inpatient. He said that since

I wasn't homicidal or suicidal or a high risk, I couldn't stay because they didn't have any beds for people like me. At the thought of going home I got more scared and agitated, so they gave me more sedatives. They allowed me to sleep in the ER for one night and then start in the partial program the next day. They said either I had to be restrained to the bed or the door to the room I was in had to be locked for safety reasons. I chose the door locked. My dad went home, my mom slept in the waiting room, and Mrs. Kreme stayed with me until 3 a.m.

The next morning I started the day program. Before I started, I talked to my dad, and he said, "Just think about this before you sign any papers, it will be on your permanent record that you had a psychiatric hospitalization. Every form you fill out you will be required to mention it." This scared me but more than anything just made me hope that I could be helped. I didn't care about my future; I cared about making it until tomorrow.

There were about eight kids, and we all sat around a table, eating bagels and drinking water. The nurse, Dan, introduced me and told everyone that I spent the night in the ER, so everyone thought I tried to kill myself. Most of the kids there had been inpatient and now were transitioning back to regular school and life. Some kids though were just in the partial program because they got referred there. We made goals for the day and then had groups. We had art group, medication group, education group, drug-education group, music group, process group, and school group Art group was the best because we got to use paints and paint whatever we wanted. Plus the art teacher, Rachel, was super nice. School was two hours a day, and it was boring because most of the kids were middle schoolers who had trouble in school, and I was a senior in high school. I mostly just helped the other kids. Process group was the first therapy I'd ever been in, and it took some getting used to. At first I just wanted to tell people that my life was none of their business, but then I learned that talking about feelings can help. Dan, the nurse, gave me a mood chart (a chart with all the moods on it) to help me identify my feelings. I was waiting for someone to say they heard voices, but no one did. I felt like I still had a big secret. I didn't like the day program, but it was less stressful than school, and whenever I got agitated, they gave me Ativan, and it calmed down the voices. A doctor was assigned to me. Dr. Kollar diagnosed me as bipolar and gave me lithium. Lithium takes a while to work to its fullest, so I didn't expect any changes. I began to read everything I could about bipolar. It sort of sounded like me, and I understood how Dr. Kollar could make that diagnosis because he didn't know everything about me.

I went to the day program from Tuesday until Friday, and then I had a weekend at home. That Saturday was my brother's bar mitzvah. My parents thought I was doing better, and they were supportive of me. They told me to ask them first if I needed anything. While I used to be able to make decisions on my own, now I had to ask my parents first. All the relatives from here to hell were in town, and we decided not to tell anyone about me being in the day program. The voices were getting worse, and on Saturday *they* started getting serious about killing me. The voices worsening combined with my overwhelming emotions was bad. *They* said *they* would make my medicine poisonous, so I stopped taking it. At the bar mitzvah I smiled and talked to everyone, but when the party came around I was tired. I didn't want to take the focus off of my brother, so I pretended I was fine. Some of my friends came by for a little while to help out, but when they left, I fell apart. I went into the bathroom and planned to kill myself. I would do it Monday morning. The voices told me how to do it, when to do it, and how good it would feel to be dead.

Once I had my plan I felt better. I slept well Saturday and Sunday night. When I woke up Monday morning, before going to the day program, I took an overdose. I took all the lithium, Ativan, Tylenol, and Robitussin. My mom drove me; even though I had my license, I wasn't allowed to drive. When I got to the hospital I wasn't hearing voices, and I realized what I had done. I went into the bathroom and tried to make myself throw up. I couldn't do it, and I panicked. *Maybe what I took won't kill me,* I thought. I couldn't risk it though; I didn't want to give up yet. I told Sarah, an MHS (mental health staff), what I had done, and she walked me immediately to the ER. By the time I was stripped and was drinking stuff to make me throw up, my parents showed up. I threw up so many times until finally they thought it was safe. My mom and dad came in, and they were shocked, again. They wanted to know when I had done it and why. I told them I had to die, I didn't want to, but I had to. They didn't understand. Once I was alive again for certain, I kind of wished I had gone through with it, especially for the first few days after. But I couldn't give up, I needed to beat this.

Somehow this time they found a bed for me in the inpatient ward. I wanted to yell at them—if they had put me in the inpatient the first time, this might have been avoided. I couldn't blame them though because I was the one who was lying. They walked me over to the inpatient unit. As we walked past the day program, all the kids yelled, "Brooke, Brooke, are you okay? We're so worried about you." The MHS wouldn't let me stop and talk so I just waved. My mom and dad weren't allowed to come into the inpatient because it wasn't visiting time, so I left them at the door and went in with the MHS. I saw Dr. Kollar, and he said he would still be my psychiatrist. He changed my medication from lithium to Zoloft. He said I was more depressed than we had originally thought. He didn't understand that I was not depressed, I was acting on the voices' commands. I was weak and stupid, but I was not depressed.

The unit was shaped like a U, and my room was in the middle of the girls' side. There was brown carpet on the floors, and the walls were all white. It wasn't sterile like a medical hospital, but it was clean. There were two men who cleaned the unit. If anyone was caught messing up the unit on purpose, they got room restricted. This means that they had to stay in their room all day. Even their meals were brought to their room. When I arrived on the unit on December 5, 1998, the entire ward was on room restriction. There had been an incident where someone, or a group of people, had stolen a fork from the meal trays and carved anarchy signs in the walls in three different areas of the hall. No one admitted doing it so everyone had to be punished. My first meeting with the group was a discussion trying to get someone to admit to carving on the walls. The staff even said that if the person admitted it, they would not be fined for damages, but if they got caught or got told on, they would have to pay for the walls to be repaired.

I couldn't imagine why someone didn't just speak up, but no one did so they were all sent back to their rooms for the rest of the day. The kids all looked nice, but I was afraid that they were going to hurt me or trick me because I was new. I acquainted myself with the unit while everyone was in their rooms. They asked why I was out, but the staff knew that I didn't do it because I had just arrived. Coming from my suicide attempt, all I wanted to do was lie down and die. Lou, a staff man, only allowed me ten minutes in my room to rest. I didn't have a roommate, but every two rooms share a bathroom. By dinner time I had spent way too much time getting to know the staff. They kept asking me why I wanted to die. I would just get all upset because I couldn't tell them. Lou told me that he thought I would do well on the unit and that was the kind of encouragement that I needed. Finally the other kids were let out. If they hadn't let them out all day then the kids would be restless when bedtime came around.

The other kids on the unit were interesting. There was a thirteen-year-old satanic girl who dressed in all black and didn't eat. She was put in because her parents were afraid of her. There was another thirteen-year-old girl who came from prison, and I never quite got her story. Each of these girls had a boyfriend on the unit. The boys were either depressed or hyperactive. There was a nineteen-year-old girl who was afraid of everything and was very violent. I was easygoing, so after I had been there for a few days, they assigned her as my roommate. There was a seventeen-year-old boy, who became a good friend, who thought he was a female and tried to kill himself out of guilt. My best friend on the unit was an eleven-year-old boy who was bipolar and very violent and explosive. He loved it when I paid attention to him, and I found him to be nonjudgmental. The information packet said the average stay was five nights, and I think that was about accurate. I was there for eight weeks. I saw lots of people come and go—runaways, depressed kids, manic kids, hyperactive kids, kids with anxiety or panic attacks, and one other kid who was psychotic.

My favorite part of the day was when people on a high-enough level got to go outside and play basketball. I was never on a high-enough level, but eventually I convinced Dr. Kollar to write an order for me to go outside with the group as long as I signed a contract. The level system worked so that if I was well behaved for three days, I could apply to move up a level, and then the group would vote on whether I should get to move up or not. I usually got voted to move up to level one which is the first level, but as soon as I cut myself, or had an episode where I needed to be locked up in the quiet room, I would be moved down to safety level. I spent most of my time on safety level, which meant that I had fewer privileges than some people who had only been on the unit for twenty-four hours. At the time, I didn't really care about privileges; I was more focused on staying alive. When I became agitated and confused, I was a threat to my own safety as well as other people's. I remember one incident where I got a pair of scissors in art and became agitated and tried to cut off my hand. Usually when this happened I would be put in the quiet room where I would scream and cry. Sometimes in the quiet room I would just huddle in a silent ball in the corner. If I still tried to hurt myself, I would be put in five-point restraints. I was slippery and could get out easily so they taped towels around my hands. Being in restraints feels terrible. I don't know how to describe it. It makes me feel like I am worth nothing when I am lying with only a hospital gown covering me and with a camera on the wall, and my body tied down unable to move. To avoid the situation where I get so upset, the staff came up with a new level called "Stuck Like Glue" or SLG as they called it to avoid embarrassing me. I was the only one on this level, and it meant that I had to go everywhere with a staff member, even to the bathroom. I had to eat with plastic utensils, and I had to sleep with my door open with a staff member right outside my door.

Meanwhile, they were messing with my medications. I was on lithium, then Zoloft, then Paxil, then Remeron, then Depakote, then Risperdal, then Wellbutrin, then finally Zyprexa. Zyprexa knocked me out and made me gain weight, but, at a high-enough dose, it sedated me enough so that I wasn't able to act out. Soon my jeans were getting snug so I had to ask my mom to bring me some sweat suits I started eating all the food they gave me on the dinner tray, even if it was gross. The apple pie was my favorite. Aside from eating, being in the quiet room, and sleeping, the rest of my day was spent in groups.

It started in the morning with "check-in." We went around in a circle, and everyone had to agree to "contract for safety," and each person also had to state his or her goal for the day. The goals had to be therapeutic. An example of what my goal might have been is "I will tell the staff if I start to hear voices" or "I will make it through school without getting distracted." Then at the end of the shift (3 p.m.), we went around in a circle and rated how well we did on meeting out goals. As I mentioned above, my favorite group was art group. The therapy groups were helpful, but I wasn't quite ready for therapy so I just asked everyone else questions. Some people thought I sounded like a therapist. They asked me how I could be so sick sometimes and so healthy the next day. I told them that was just the nature of my illness. Anyway, back to art group, when I was able to concentrate enough to do a project, I always had fun drawing and painting. The leader, Rachel, was very patient and never yelled. I think she was one of the few people who understood me. In between group activities more kids could go to their room or the common room for five minutes, but I had to sit next to the nurses' station in a brown chair. Everyone called it Brooke's chair, and no one else ever sat in it besides me. That brown chair got to be a place I could go if I was feeling sad, scared, or confused, and I would be allowed to sit without being interrogated.

I was very secretive about my problems. I was in the hospital because I tried to kill myself, so everyone thought I was depressed. But, to them, I looked healthy. So, my diagnosis was bipolar disorder. I didn't tell anyone about the voices until I had been there for about three weeks. I told a nurse, Nellie. She said, "Is something wrong?" and I said, "Yes, I hear voices that no one else hears." Once I had told her that, it was much easier to talk to her about the visual hallucinations, the fearfulness, and the confusion. We had a long conversation. I was so scared because I had never told anyone before I thought either she wouldn't believe me or she would try to kill me. But, it turned out okay. The nurse, Nellie, told Dr. Kollar about my psychosis, and that's when he prescribed Zyprexa. I took Zyprexa every day, and as I said, it made me gain weight, and it sedated me. Plus, I was still "depressed." When I went back on Zoloft it made me hyper, and it made my voices worse. So I went back on lithium. When that didn't help enough with my moods (I still was depressed), I went on Depakote too.

With all those meds, I couldn't concentrate enough to do any of the schoolwork that was sent from my school, so I mostly helped my younger friends with theirs. I got along well with the staff because I was cooperative, and they understood that even though I was sometimes out of control, it wasn't my fault. There was one incident when I stole a plastic knife and cut myself with it. When the other kids saw how much attention I got for that, they all started stealing knives. I felt terrible that I had caused such a problem, and I apologized and took the responsibility, even though I was acting on what the voices asked me to do.

At nighttime if I couldn't sleep I was allowed to hang out with the staff until I got tired. They encouraged me to walk in circles around the unit until I got sleepy. I got to spend some time with the other boy who was psychotic. His psychosis was different; he had episodes every other night at 8 p.m. where he had visual hallucinations and got scared until it passed in about an hour. His psychosis started when he fell off a cliff skiing and got a head injury. We related well to each other though because we were somehow "different."

Once the other kids found out about my voices, most of them were supportive. One boy wanted to show me his collection of articles and photographs of serial killers because that's how he thought of people who hear voices. Another girl started trying to help me every time I sat in the brown chair; she wanted to be my personal assistant through the rough times, but the problem was she was trying to be a caretaker of everyone else but was not taking care of herself.

Since I was there for so long, all the staff knew me well, and soon they were able to tell by looking at me when I needed Ativan and when I needed to go into the quiet room. I felt very safe while I was there, even though I managed to hurt myself a few times. My friends from school knew where I was, and they sent me letters every day. Mrs. Kreme came to visit me every day, and she brought the letters. She went into all my classes with my brother and talked to my classmates about me being in the hospital. My parents also came to visit me every day. They brought me dinner. At first they had a lot of questions, and they thought I didn't need to be in the hospital, but soon they got used to it. My parents were confused because most kids show warning signs before they get hospitalized, but for me it was sudden. I hid all the warning signs.

One day four of the kids on the unit got all dressed up in all of their clothes and shoes (without shoelaces), and they even put on makeup. I asked them why they were dressed to go outside, thinking that they were going to get an MRI or something, and they told me it was none of my business. So I backed off. That night the four kids tried to escape; they threw a chair through a window in the middle of the night. The chair must have been heavy because it's hard to break thick Plexiglas. They had to go past the nurses' station to get to the window, so one boy ran around in the adult's rooms and pressed all the emergency help buttons. Then, once the nurses were engaged in helping all the people who called for them, the kids were able to sneak by. At the last minute the nurses found them, but the kids had already gotten away. They ran toward the highway and stopped for a break under the bridge. Hospital security found them, and they were initially brought back to the hospital.

One of them got sent home, one got sent to the state hospital, Fairfax, and two got to stay. One of those who got to stay was a little mentally retarded, and the staff thought that she was just doing it to be cool. The other one was new to the unit; she had only been there three days, and she had nowhere to go. She had been moving from house to house, and finally they found her a bed in a hospital so they were going to let her keep it. I thought they all should have been sent away. We had a meeting, and it turned out that everyone except me knew that they were going to run. We all got room restricted for not telling on people who were engaging in dangerous behavior. The whole situation was sad, because they should have been getting better if they had stayed.

It was encouraging to see people getting better, and there was a joke that the hospital was going to hire me since I had been there so long. Finally after about seven weeks I was getting better; I was off of safety level on level 1, and I hadn't been in restraints for a week. Dr. Kollar was convinced that my meds were keeping me safe. The problem was that they were also making me ravenous and exhausted. My parents questioned every move that the hospital made. The social worker thought I was ready to be discharged but was not ready to go back to school or back home. He recommended that I get sent to a residential treatment center for girls in Montana. There was a waiting list to get in so I would have to stay in the hospital for a while longer. He also said that Overlake Hospital had an RTC so I decided to go there. I did not want to go to Montana. At that point I couldn't worry about anything or anyone else beside myself, so I did what was in my best interest. I wanted to be able to finish school, no matter what it took; I wanted to graduate with my class.

I took a tour of the RTC. There was only one patient there, my eleven-year-old friend from the inpatient unit. He was so excited that I might be coming. I figured I would be able to get some of my schoolwork done there, they could monitor my meds, and my parents could visit every day. I decided to go to the RTC.

I didn't have many clothes with me, so I put them in a bag with my stuffed dog, Muttsy, and I walked with an MHS over to the new unit. It had more freedom; we were allowed to go for walks and go to the cafeteria. The groups were basically the same, except with different leaders. I had my own room, but I spent most of my free time out on the ward playing ping-pong with George, my little friend. During school I tried to read, but my teacher had sent *The Mahabharata*, and I couldn't focus on it. Group therapy was kind of like individual therapy with a person watching because there were only two of us. They gave candy rewards for everything which only helped me gain weight. George and I made a deal as to which day each of us would win the cleanest room award. We actually had fun; it was much less stressful than the hospital because I was feeling better.

One night I even helped Leo, one of the staff, with his physics homework from the University of Washington. My brain was coming back to me, and I was excited. After I had been there for one week with just one other patient, two new patients came— one fourteen-year-old girl and one fifteen-year-old boy. The boy and I became good friends, but it was hard to talk to the girl because she was angry. She had a drug problem that she was trying to get help for, but the drug treatment facility sent her to the RTC for treatment of her eating disorder. She barely ate and fainted often. I was scared for her.

But the boy, Niles, was trying really hard. He also had bipolar disorder, and he had been through a lot. I kept in touch with him, but it was too hard because he was in and out of jail, and his family was with the military, and they were constantly moving. One time I saw him on a talk show on TV for kids who are out of control. He was in a situation very similar to mine, but he was using drugs which made him a lot worse off. I was in the RTC for two weeks, and in retrospect I think I would have been able to make the transition fine without it. When I got out of the RTC, I tried to go to the Partial Day Program, but it was overwhelming because I had all these memories about how I used to be, so I just went home and back to school. I transferred out of my honors classes, except AP Biology, and I joined my lacrosse team midseason.

I was too out of shape to run so I became the goalie, which was fun. At school, no one treated me differently; it was as though I'd never been gone. However, I couldn't read as fast or type as fast as before, so my work took more time. I started to see a therapist, Laurel, and I continued to see Dr. Kollar. I also continued to see Mrs. Kreme at school.

Going to therapy became part of my week; I didn't like it at first, but then I started to feel like Laurel really understood me and could help me. I had a lot of secrets that I needed help exploring and sharing.

I started going to the gym and working out to try to lose weight. The weight I put on from Zyprexa, Depakote, and lithium was hard to lose. We constantly thought about changing my meds. I saw a bipolar specialist, and he said I needed them all, so I stayed on them. I didn't know about any other antipsychotic meds besides Zyprexa and Risperdal, which I had tried once with no results.

My family acted like I was never gone; they even let me start driving again after a few weeks. My schoolwork was challenging, but not too hard. During my hospitalization, I had applied to college. I was wait listed at six colleges and rejected from one. Here is my college application essay. I literally wrote this from inside the quiet room.

12/17/97

I had thought the pills would kill me. After all, I had taken about fifty of them. But, on December 1, when I tried to commit suicide, there was a part of me that did not want to die. Luckily for me, the part of me that wanted to live was able to break through the confused net of my mind and tell someone that I had taken an overdose and needed help.

Now, December 17, I am writing this personal statement from the Overlake Hospital Adolescent Psychiatric Ward. I will remain here, at the hospital, until I am safe enough to go back home into my regular life. I know that I will reach a point of stability, but for now I am confused and frustrated.

Although I would like to say that suicide was a one-try kind of thing for me, I cannot deny the intensity of the force inside me. In the past, this force has given me the energy to excel past all boundaries. Recently though, the force has made me feel like I need to kill myself. At the hospital, I have had to be put in five-point leather restraints to keep me from harming myself.

My doctor and the unit's staff are committed to figuring out what's wrong. They don't understand how I can have so much self-confidence, so much pride in myself and my future, and yet I still feel the need to kill myself. I have been put on antidepressants, sleeping pills, and some other medicines to help clarify my thoughts and to help the voices in my head not be so loud and demanding. In a couple of weeks, once enough gets into my system, I will see if the medications provide any relief. Until then, I know that I must not comply with what my mind keeps telling me to do. This is a task which is easier said than done, but I know I can do it.

It frustrates me that my overdose has caused my friends and family so much grief. I feel bad because my wanting to die makes other people feel like I do not care about them. But my compassion is sincere. It is just hard for me to explain how, when I feel like I need to kill myself, no matter how much I love other people, it is not enough to stop me from harming myself.

My grades might suffer due to my absence at school, but all my teachers and I agree that it is okay. Right now my priority is to take care of myself. Whether it is through the joy I provide to my family, the community service I provide by helping others, or just the positive aura I give off, I know that the world is a better place with me. For now, by keeping myself at the hospital, I am keeping myself safe. The people here will not let me kill myself, and I am glad.

Now, I have learned more about psychology and neuroscience than I ever intended to learn in my entire life. I have also learned a lot about the virtues of patience. It is hard for me to wait this out, because I am constantly wanting to understand why and how. But, getting frustrated will not help me survive. The motto here around the hospital is What Doesn't Kill You Only Makes You Stronger, and I can apply that to myself. By surviving this mental trauma of wanting to live yet needing to die at the same time, I will be stronger. I will understand mental illness in a way that I never could have before, and hopefully, one day, I will be able to help ease other's mental trauma in the medical field.

Although it may seem odd that I would write about what most would consider a flaw in my otherwise perfectly knit seventeen-year-old existence, this seems like all I am able to focus on right now. I am trying to portray my courage and perseverance, but I don't know how when right at this instant I am feeling like I need to kill myself.

I can't judge, but if my counselor didn't have to write a letter saying that I was in the hospital, and if I had been more subtle in my approach, I might have been accepted at more schools. I was disappointed not to get into college but not surprised, considering how sick I had been and probably still would be if I wasn't so medicated. But, I really wanted to go to college, so I wrote a letter explaining how much better I was doing, and I got accepted. Aside from being overweight and sleeping about sixteen hours a day, my symptoms were mild, and I was just happy that I was alive.

At the end of April though, my symptoms started to come back strongly. The voices started telling me that I should kill myself, and *they* were very angry. I told Laurel, and she said maybe I needed a break in the hospital.

CHAPTER 5

Saltines and Apple Juice

I sat in the conference room that had an anarchy sign carved into the wall with a fork. I guessed it had never gotten fixed. Usually when I was admitted to the psychiatric ward I had to go through a long tedious interview in the emergency room. This time I bypassed the emergency room admitting psychiatrist because Laurel called the unit and told them I was coming. I sat in the stark white conference room facing the window to the unit. It smelled like cleaning solution. I didn't want to look at my mom. I was embarrassed that she had to bring me back here. I always heard her telling her friends that I was getting better. Now with this setback I felt like a failure. One of the night nurses came in and took away my shoelaces and my belt.

"Do you have anything sharp or any drugs on you?" the nurse asked.

"No," I replied.

"I promise to do a strip search later on," the nurse teased. I was not in the mood for teasing, especially about a strip search. It entailed taking off all of my clothes and letting her check them for sharps and drugs. The nurse doing the strip search checked every seam and pocket to make sure I wasn't hiding anything. They sometimes even made me lift up my breasts and spread my arms and legs to make sure I wasn't hiding anything. During my last hospital stay, when I somehow always found things to cut myself with, they had to do strip searches daily. This was especially hard for me because I couldn't deal with people touching me. As soon as I heard the words "Put your arms out to the side and spread your legs," I sort of dissociated into a place where I was watching from the outside instead of being myself. I shut my eyes and hoped it would be over as soon as possible. I only hid a razor blade one time. I found it on the bathroom floor, so it either belonged to my roommate or the girls next door. I stole some alcohol pads from the first aid kit by asking for some athletic tape to tape my feet. The nurse who gave it to me looked away from the first aid kit for one second, and I grabbed several alcohol pads. I cleaned the razor and then taped it to the bottom of my shampoo bottle so I could cut myself in the shower. A female staff person usually watched me shower, but oftentimes she would just stick her head in and check every few minutes. When I got out and was bleeding they eventually figured out that I was cutting in the shower because they were watching me every other second.

Because I was not the only one who was sneaking in contraband, they also did room searches. These searches were not only for sharps, but also for drugs and food, which we were not allowed to have.

The nurse asked my mom to leave and told her that they would take care of me. I bid my mom goodbye, and I told her that if I killed myself I would want her to read my diary. "Brooke, you will not kill yourself while you're in here, and we won't let you out until you are safe," the nurse responded automatically. After my mom left, I looked up and recognized one of the nurses from my last stay at Overlake Hospital.

I didn't know if the nurse, Denise, knew I was there. I hoped she would also recognize me from some of the long nights we had spent together in the quiet room. Denise turned and looked, and I smiled. She came running over. "I'm so glad to see you, and I am so glad that you are safe," Denise touched my hand just enough for me to feel her presence. I felt a little better when I saw her, I think because I associated her with safety. She asked about the voices, and when I didn't answer she knew I needed Ativan. That first night was a night from hell. I was so suicidal that all I could think about was every possible way to kill myself in the inpatient psychiatric ward. I feel obligated not to list these ways for anyone who might think to use this as a pocket guide of how to kill yourself in a psych ward, but there were many ways.

I couldn't sleep because the voices were keeping me up. *"You're so weak you can't even kill yourself; you just run back to the little hospital when you get close to doing it. Why don't you kill yourself right now before they start watching you like a hawk again? You are so stupid and selfish. All you care about is yourself. The world would be so much better without you"*

There was a chair that I used to sit on in my last hospitalization, a brown recliner. I went right to the chair as soon as I was allowed on the unit. I knew it was going to be a long, hard night because the voices were loud, and *they* were set on the fact that I was going to die. I was sitting in the chair when suddenly I blinked, and I was lying in the quiet room tied down to the bed in five-point leather restraints. The nurses were watching me on the television monitor, and when I woke up, Denise came in to talk to me. I asked what had happened, and she said that I had a psychotic episode. She asked if I was still hearing voices. I told her yes, but I wanted to know more about what had happened; it's scary to wake up in restraints and not know how you got there. All Denise would tell me was that I got very confused and had to be restrained by security in order to ensure my safety. I felt a little better, but they wouldn't take the restraints off until I proved to them that I was calm for one hour. The restraints were leather, and they were buckled around each ankle, each wrist, and my waist. The leather was worn from being stretched around so many people's limbs. I had towels taped around my hands and feet, which led me to believe that I had been struggling to pull my hands and feet through the restraints. I was lying on a thin foam mattress with a plastic pillow under my head. A hospital gown covered me, and I knew I had my underwear on under it because I could feel the elastic around my hips. I could turn my head to both sides. The room was kind of padded, but not really. It hurt when I slammed my head into the wall, which I had tried once. The ceiling was too high for me to touch, even if I jumped.

The light was in the middle of the ceiling and was covered with a screen. The room was adequately clean. There was one window, but I couldn't see it from where I lay tied to the bed. The window was up at the top behind my head. There was a video camera, not even disguised, that was focused right on the bed. The mattress was on top of two metal bars, one on each side for the straps to hook around. There was a series of two doors that one had to go through to get into the quiet room. The outer door was metal and locked like a vault with a big wheel. The inner door was wooden but padded on the inside. There was a window big enough for me to see through to the metal door. When I was tied down I couldn't see out of the windows or doors.

The nurses took me out of the restraints little by little. First one leg came out for an hour, then one leg and one arm.

After I got out of restraints I spent the rest of the night in my new room. All the kids were different, but most of the staff were the same. The next day my doctor decided to reevaluate my meds once more. He tried me on Risperdal, an antipsychotic similar to Zyprexa. I was on it for about five days, and it didn't work at all. When I was on Risperdal it felt like I was unmedicated. I heard voices all the time. There were many of *them* doing a running commentary on my life, judging if what I was doing met their standards. I was constantly confused about who I was, who the nurses were, who my parents were, and why I couldn't go outside. One time I did get outside. All I remember is being brought back in by about five big men dressed in black (security) who actually picked me up and carried me. The nurses had a camera at every door, and I don't remember how I got out. Obviously I was too confused and hallucinating too much to stay on Risperdal. I had tried it during my last hospitalization, and it hadn't worked then either. I willingly went back to Zyprexa. I think they increased my dose. I was exhausted all the time, and I was getting to be obese. When the other kids went outside to play basketball, I sat on the sofa and ate saltines and drank apple juice. I talked to my teachers from school about the work I was missing because I desperately wanted to graduate with my class in two months to prove to myself that I was normal. While the other kids in the unit did word searches during school, I read *The Mahabharata*. While the other kids played pool, I wrote essays about politics in Russia. I was working hard to get out of the hospital as soon as possible, but a fear was building up inside me that I would never be able to stay out of the hospital. I saw the adults on the unit, and I was scared that I would be one of them. They shared a unit with us, but we barely saw them except in the hallways.

Every night the scary people came out and tried to attack me. I tried to practice my breathing-relaxation techniques, but nothing worked except Ativan. One night I had eight milligrams of Ativan in two hours. Finally I started to feel better. Laurel came to see me in the hospital, and she said I was looking better and sounding more connected to reality. All the other kids were nice; they just thought I was weird. I heard them talking about me when I was out of the room. "That girl's insane. Just seeing her makes me feel better about myself. She's so weird." I felt sad that I couldn't be a part of the camaraderie that the other patients formed with each other. When I heard them say I was weird, I started to feel more and more weird myself.

On my fourth night there I felt a little better, and I was able to sleep in my room for the whole night. I woke up to my friend Connor standing above me. I met Connor the last time I was hospitalized, and now he was back at the same time. He had heard I was here, and he snuck into my room. He had tried to kill himself again. Connor was a homosexual, and every time he got intimate with a guy he started hating himself so much for being gay that he would try to kill himself. I asked him how serious it was, and he said if no one had walked in on him he would have bled to death. I got up and gave Connor a big hug. I was glad to see someone who understood me, but I wished he wasn't so sick. Last time when we met I showed Connor the letter I used to come out in my high school newspaper, and he made a copy to show his friends. I was insecure about my sexuality too, but I was open minded to whatever might happen, unlike Connor who couldn't bear the thought of being gay.

I was getting a lot of attention (in the form of rules and restrictions) because I was so fragile and confused. My actions were being determined by the voices. Finally the nurses who saw me all day convinced Dr. Kollar that I needed more meds so he raised my Zyprexa to 25 mg, a dose so high that it had not been tested on children yet. Within two days I was tired and hungry, but the voices were fading, and my confusion was wearing off. I stayed out of restraints for three days. Because the psychosis got me so much attention and the Zyprexa made me feel so much better, Connor started seeing things and hearing voices. Maybe it's true that Connor suddenly started having hallucinations, but more likely he was imitating something that he liked.

His doctor treated him just like any psychotic patient and gave him meds and moved his level down to ISOS. After a day I couldn't stand hearing everything I say repeated by Connor so I told the nurse what I thought was happening, and she confronted Connor. He denied everything. Soon though, he wasn't able to play his guitar because of the side effects of Zyprexa so he quit taking it, and his hallucinations never came back.

I got released on a Monday, and I slowly integrated myself back into school. My schedule was International Studies, English, and AP Biology. I got independent study in psychology in order to have enough credits to graduate. School was okay, but I was so tired I could barely stay awake. I passed all my classes with A's and Bs, and that was all I really cared about. I used to go to school with motivation to learn and expand my mind, but I was feeling rather hopeless at the end of my senior year. All I wanted to do was graduate.

I got an E-mail from Connor one day. Connor had already graduated from high school. He wanted to get together and have lunch outside of the hospital. I knew that Connor used heroin, and I didn't want to be exposed to that so I changed my AOL screen name. He found me. He called me on the phone and e-mailed me every day. When I got the courage I wrote him a long E-mail about how I didn't want to see him because of his drug use and his insecurity. I explained how it was me and not him that was crazy, but I still didn't want to see him. With that note I think I knocked Connor off the edge of the earth. I never heard from him again. I called him—no answer. I called his parents— they said he couldn't come to the phone. I didn't know what happened to him, and I couldn't allow myself to feel guilty. Finally when I saw him on-line one day I agreed to meet for lunch. He was allowed to drive so he picked me up at my house, and we went to Kirkland, a nearby city, for lunch. He offered me drugs and thank God I had the sense to refuse him. He took me home and told me when he dropped me off that he was going to kill himself. I ignored the threat, but I shouldn't have. I called his number (which was a 1-800 number), and his friend answered. He told me that Connor had killed himself. I didn't know how to feel. We were very similar, Connor and I, but the drugs separated us. I was never and never will be an addict like Connor was. Still, I was tortured by his death; I lost a friend to suicide. That was a tough thing for me to deal with I didn't tell anyone except Laurel. I didn't want any of my friends to know because they would pity me, and I didn't want anyone to say, "Oh, poor Brooke, her friend died." I wanted to be strong.

I went about my life, and I graduated from high school. I felt healthy except for my sleepiness and constant hunger. To this day I don't have any idea what I did all summer, and I can't find evidence of my doing anything. Maybe I was working, maybe I went to school. It obviously wasn't very memorable. When August came around I abandoned all hope of going to Williams College, the school I had planned to attend. I became so hopeless that I declared, "If I can't go to college, I don't want to live." I wanted so badly to have my life back, the life where no one knew anything was wrong and I was in control. Now, I was way out of control, and it was scary. My therapist interpreted my hopelessness as suicidality and asked me to go to the hospital. My parents interfered, claiming that Overlake Hospital was doing nothing for me. They proposed I either go to Children's Hospital or University of Washington Medical Center. I chose UWMC; I didn't want to be with little kids. I wanted to be a responsible grown-up.

CHAPTER 6

Boston Calls

One old woman sat in the hallway, moaning. The nurses put her there in the morning. She moaned all day. It sounded like she was saying, "I have to go to the bathroom." Whenever I told the nurses that, they promised me that she was okay, and they had just taken her to the bathroom. At night, they usually moved her back to her bed. One evening I walked by, and she wasn't moaning. I looked at her closely, and she was slumped to the left. I told the nurse that the old woman didn't look well, and within minutes I heard, *"Code Red 4N, Code Red 4N."* About ten doctors came rushing in and took her away on a stretcher. I think the woman had a heart attack. When I asked they said it was none of my business. The nurses at UWMC were not very nice. The UWMC was an adult psych ward unlike the adolescent psych ward I had been in at Overlake Hospital. At eighteen, I was the youngest patient. There were no groups, no staff people around to talk to, and there was no structure.

I was there because of my suicidality, and I wasn't allowed any visitors except for two hours each evening. Having no visitors all day made me even lonelier. I spent the days looking at the adults, most of whom were receiving ECT, and hoping that I would not become like them. My doctor, Dr. Dwib, was weird. He diagnosed me with rapid-cycling bipolar disorder, although he told me that he was not 100 percent confident with his diagnosis. He put me on lithium, Depakote, and Zyprexa. He gave me Dalmane to help me sleep but refused to let me have Ativan as a PRN.

After one week I was feeling a little better, and I needed to get outside, so I asked to be discharged. Dr. Dwib discharged me and told me to continue going to therapy and taking meds. I asked him if he thought I would be able to go to college in January (it was August), and he said it would be a very long time before I was ready to go to school. All I wanted to do was to feel better and go to college like my brother had done and like all my friends were about to do. But the doctor said no.

I had a meeting with Dr. Kollar (my psychiatrist), Laurel, and my parents. I wanted to discuss when I could go to school, and they wanted to discuss what I would do to keep myself busy so I wouldn't get depressed. When I was on 25 mg Zyprexa, I did not get psychotic. I decided that I would defer my admission to Williams College for one year, and in the meantime I would sign up for courses at the community college. I did not want to go to Williams halfway through the year because it would be too hard to make friends and fit in. I signed up for psychology and biology at Bellevue Community College.

All my friends went off to college, none within driving distance of my house. I was lonely, and I talked to Laurel in therapy about what to do with loneliness. My solution was to cut myself, and she didn't like that. One afternoon I was home with my brother Phil, and I went to the store, bought a pack of single-edged blades, and attacked my left arm. After an hour, when two of the cuts wouldn't stop bleeding, I decided to call Laurel and ask for help. She told me to come to her office immediately so she could assess the damages. She told me to take Phil with me. When we got there, she decided that I didn't need stitches, and she asked me to wait for her to finish with two more clients, and then we would talk. I sat in the waiting room, bleeding all over the place for two hours. Every twenty minutes Laurel came out to check on me. As I sat there I began losing touch with reality. Usually the Zyprexa prevented the psychosis, but this time I was hearing voices. *They* told me to run, but I just sat there. When she was done with all her appointments, Laurel took Phil and me home, and she said either she had to stay at our house or we had to go to the hospital. I chose to have her stay at our house until my parents got home that night because I hated the hospital more than anything.

After that I began cutting more frequently. My classes were going well in terms of grades, but I slept through them every day. To take up my time I would draw, write, and go to the gym. I always worked out hard, but I never lost weight. I had been on Zyprexa for a year, and I had gained seventy pounds. I wanted to do something exciting so I signed up for an outward-bound trip. The trip was a "dog sledding in Minnesota" adventure. As soon as they found out about my medications they disqualified me. The semester ended, and I had two weeks off before the next semester started so I asked my dad to take me skiing.

I used to be an excellent skier, but the additional seventy pounds made me slower and more tired. The ski trip turned into a sleep-and-eat trip with a little bit of skiing. I still had fun though; it was the first time I had gone skiing all year.

I got back at school just in time to start multivariable calculus and drawing. I was fearful that I was going to end up graduating from community college and not even going to a four-year college or university. I wanted to be a doctor, and all my plans were getting ruined. Everyone I talked to told me to just be patient, and I would get better, but I was getting impatient, I felt like crap, and I wanted to get better immediately.

My parents saw that I was becoming increasingly sick with more suicidality, anger, and cutting. The meds were not effective. I was working on identifying emotions, but I couldn't even tell the doctors how I felt or if I was depressed. I was so used to keeping my emotions on a flat line that now I had to figure out what they all were like. We had a family meeting, and my doctor said that he didn't know what to do to help me. I was stuck. Our only choice was to get reevaluated.

My parents were scared that I was going to die. I had so much potential, and my parents saw it, and they did not want me to lose everything I had worked so hard to get and keep up until this point. My dad looked up psychiatric hospitals on the

Internet and found the two best-ranked hospitals and called them. He asked about my specific situation and how they would be able to help me. Both hospitals suggested a complete start over to get all the old drugs that aren't working out of my system and then try something new. I chose McLean Hospital just outside Boston, Massachusetts, because if I went there they would put me in an adolescent residential treatment facility with other kids up to age twenty-one. If I went to the other hospital, I would be put in a locked adult ward, and I would have been one of the younger ones in the unit.

I was excited about trying something new. I was sick of being stuck in the same old rut. The thought of getting better was so enticing to me that I didn't even care about moving across the country. My mom took me to McLean for the first time. We met with Cici, the head of the program; Dwight, my case manager; and Dr. Wilts, my new psychiatrist. I had to give a lot of details about the symptoms I experienced, and Cici kept telling me that I might not be able to stay there if I got psychotic. The unit was not equipped to deal with people who hear voices or cut themselves. The unit was unlocked so I could technically leave at any time, although I signed a contract to stay. The kids had to cook for themselves so there were kitchen utensils and appliances around. I told Cici that I needed to try, and I would promise to tell the staff if I didn't think I was safe. I signed a safety contract, and they showed me my room.

My roommate, Julie, had OCD (obsessive-compulsive disorder), and the room was very clean. She liked to have everything clean. The kids there were nice, and I felt like I had people to talk to for the first time in a while. I met with Dr. Wilts every day, and he immediately started decreasing the dosage of my meds. That was fine for about three days, but then I went into an extreme psychotic episode. I don't remember anything. I was in the ART (adolescent residential treatment) with lots of people around me, and then I blinked, and I was in a quiet room with my wrists all bandaged.

Soon, Dr. Wilts showed up and explained to me that I was

acting unsafe and I had hurt myself so they had sent me over to NB2 (North Belknap Two), an inpatient floor. Dr. Wilts told me that they were going to get me back to the ART as soon as possible. He told me that he had referred me to his friend who deals with a lot of childhood psychosis and he wanted her to evaluate me when I got back to the ART. I stayed on NB2 for about a week until I could function on my own without the voices interfering. I was determined to get out of NB2 because I thought the doctor there was trying to kill me. He was giving me random pills and demanding that I take them. He was poisoning my food. He was going to kill me the instant he got alone with me. I had to get out.

When I went back to the ART, East House, several people had left, and several new people had come. I got a new room and a new roommate. Dr. Wilts took me over to meet Dr. Fluten, the specialist, and I liked her. Her office was full of toys. She was dressed casually but nice enough to look respectable. She had a habit of running her fingers through her hair that made me feel like she was interested in what I was saying. I only met her for a few minutes, and she promised to come over to East House to see me.

During the time I spent at East House I went to lots of groups, basically the same sort of groups that I had at Overlake hospital. We had a women's group, a process group, and then some different ones like skills group and psychodrama. Skills group was for everyone who had trouble managing life because they lacked skills like communication, dealing with emotions, and interpersonal skills. It was basically a group modeled after DBT (dialectical behavior therapy). I liked skills group because I felt like I was actually learning something that could help me. Psychodrama, on the other hand, I hated. We mostly just played games, but every once in a while someone volunteered to do a psychodrama about his or her life. This basically entailed acting out a problem using other people as objects and characters in your life. An old man ran a psychodrama, and he was always touching people. Since I hated being touched, I tried to stay as far away from him as possible.

Another big difference between the ART at McLean and the hospital in Seattle was that we had real school at McLean. We had three classes and had to rotate among them. I had already graduated from high school, so for me the school at East House was a waste of time. I wish they would have allowed me to read my book, but the teachers insisted on interfering. Some days I couldn't go to school because I was too agitated and distracted; those days I spent the schooltime sitting in a chair, staring at a wall. They didn't know what to do with me. Eventually they let me read and draw pictures, other times they asked me to write in a journal, and then they read what I wrote. For other kids it worked well, but for me it was a waste. I tried not to distract other kids.

At East House there were residential patients who stayed there twenty-four hours a day like me, and then there were day students who came at 8:30 a.m. and left at 4:00 p.m. The day students were generally healthier than the residentials. Many people used the day program as a transition to get from the inpatient ward back to school and home life. Because there were day students, we were not allowed to go into our rooms during the day. This bothered me because sometimes I felt like taking a rest on my bed, and I wasn't allowed to. Also, much to my surprise, patients were allowed to smoke. As long as it wasn't too late at night, the doors were unlocked, and we were allowed to go out into the fenced-in backyard. People could run away and on occasion did. But, for most of the time, no one ran away because they knew they would get caught.

There were two tracks at East House: skills track and substance-abuse track. This is how it seemed to me. We all did most things together except for the DBT (dialectical behavior therapy) groups and the substance-abuse groups. Also, three nights a week all the substance abusers went to AA meetings. They liked it because they could stop and buy cigarettes, but I'm glad I never had to go. Except once.

East House was into doing random drug testing because they thought people could sneak drugs in somehow. In order to be fair they had to test everyone, not just the people who were known to use drugs. One day they asked me to pee in a cup, and I said no. I hate peeing in a cup, and there was no reason for them to suspect me of using drugs. They said if I didn't go I would be treated as if my test had come back positive. I said fine. So, they rearranged my whole schedule, put me in the drug group, and asked me to go to an AA meeting. I went along with it because I honestly was only at East House to try out some new meds and stay in a safe environment. Anything I learned while I was there was a plus. After about three days of having me in the substance-abuse tract they realized it was ridiculous, and they sent me back to the DBT tract. I was scared that they were going to find out about how I used to use speed recreationally, but they didn't seem to care.

Dr. Fluten came to see me a few times. Often when she came I was having an episode or not communicating. When she came, we talked in the TV room. She wanted to have me thoroughly evaluated so I could get a current diagnosis and make sure there was nothing physically wrong with my brain. Until the testing was done, I was surviving on a low dose of Zyprexa and lots of Ativan to keep me calm.

Meanwhile I was participating in groups at East House and socializing with the other kids. I made a few friends, but to this day I only keep in touch with one girl, Bara. Bara seemed to have every problem there was, but I think she had an eating disorder and depression. I could not relate to her issues, and she thought mine were weird, so we never talked about psych stuff, we just played cards. In a few days I went to get an EEG, an MRI, a blood work, and a psychological testing. I had an EEG in Seattle so I knew what it was like. They hook electrodes all over my head, and then I sit in a big comfy chair, and they flash light across my face. It was fine. Then I had an MRI which I also had in Seattle. This MRI tube was different though because it had a mirror so I could see out. The technician kept telling me not to move, and all I wanted to do was scratch my nose. I lay in the tube for about forty minutes, and then she let me out. That was fine too. Then I had the psychological testing. It wasn't the same as I had in Seattle with the Rorschach and the story tiles. It was more questions about my past that I didn't know the answer to, and then some IQ testing. After all that was done, Dr. Wilts took me and my dad to meet Dr. Fluten again. She gave me a new diagnosis of schizoaffective disorder and recommended a medication called Moban. She said I would probably have to stay on lithium to control my moods, but Moban should help with the psychosis. I looked Moban up, and it is an old antipsychotic medicine that doesn't cause as many side effects as some of the others. It was the only old antipsychotic that doesn't cause weight gain. I decided to try it.

Within two weeks I felt like a new woman. I wasn't hearing voices anymore, and that was the only thing that I cared about. All the rest of my symptoms were acceptable now that the voices were gone. I thought Moban was the miracle drug. But, of course, I was not ready to be discharged yet. I was in my room, and the staff came in and asked if I was okay. I told them I was having urges to cut myself, but I was fine, and I would be safe. I guess the staff didn't believe me because ten minutes later the security men showed up at my door ready to take me away to the CEC. The CEC is the Clinical Evaluation Center. It is where they take you if they think you need to be hospitalized. I told the security that there must have been a miscommunication because I was fine. They insisted on taking me away, and I refused to go voluntarily because I was fine. So they took me involuntarily. I sat in the CEC for five hours, and then finally they let me use the phone. I called my dad, who had just left Boston for Seattle, and I cried to him that they were locking me up for no reason. He turned right back around and flew to Boston. He missed the multiple sclerosis benefit auction that my mom was putting on. I was so proud of my mom for putting together the MS auction, and I felt so guilty for making my dad miss my mom's special moment, but I needed someone to take care of me and not let stupid people violate me. I think my mom understood that I was thinking of her even though I couldn't be there.

My mom and dad had been taking turns watching me at the hospital. One would stay for a week in a hotel, and then they would rotate. They would come to see me every day during visiting hours. My younger brother had to live with only one parent at a time in Seattle. My parents treated me better than could be imagined, and I am grateful for that.

My dad arrived in Boston at the middle of the night so he came to see me first thing in the morning. I was furious; all I wanted was to go back to East House. It's not that I really wanted to be at East House, it was just the principle of them taking me away for no reason. My dad trusted me when I said I was safe, and he talked to the doctor, and I was let out. It was my shortest hospital stay ever: one night! Back at East House I got the same bed and the same roommate. My roommate was super nice, but she was a little crazy. Two nights after I got back she decided to pierce her nose with a safety pin. She stole frozen meat from the freezer to numb her nose, and she stuck the safety pin through. It took about two hours, and every time she would scream, the staff would knock on our door, and we had to come up with some excuse. She snuck out to put the meat back at 4:00 am., and her nose was pierced. The next day it looked okay, but by the third day it was all red and nasty. She couldn't even get it out herself because her nose was too sore. That was the strangest roommate experience I had. The rest of my roommates were all fairly normal. Most of them were in the hospital for depression or drug use. A lot of them were acting out in school, or not going to school. They had big problems that were very different than mine. I have schizoaffective disorder.

I didn't really even know what it was. In process group my case manager asked how my new diagnostic process was going. I told him and the group that I got a new diagnosis of schizoaffective disorder, but I didn't really know what it meant. There was a quiet boy in the group who had schizoaffective disorder too. He told me that it meant having depression or anxiety in addition to psychosis. I thanked the boy, but I told him that it didn't sound like me. The next day Dr. Fluten came to see me, and I asked her what it meant. She asked how the Moban was working, but she could tell from my lucid state that I was feeling better. In the past she seemed to always catch me when I was hallucinating, probably because that was happening most of the time. Dr. Fluten, Dr.Wilts, and I were all pleased with the results of the Moban. Before Dr. Fluten left I asked again if she could tell me what schizoaffective meant. She said that it varies, but for me it is a mood disorder and psychosis which occur independently of each other. I wanted too look it up, but I had no book and no Internet access in East House.

I was in East House for about five weeks, and when I started getting ready to leave, there was a big question of where I would go after my discharge. Our house in Seattle was sold, but we didn't have a new house in Boston yet. My family had decided to move to Boston to be closer to good medical treatment for me. They realized that I have a serious disorder, and they wanted me to get the best treatment, which was in Boston with Dr. Fluten. My family also moved closer to my dad's business and closer to my older brother's school. We moved also because my family likes change. One choice was that I could live in a halfway house or a group home (I think these are the same thing but I'm not sure). Another choice was to rent an apartment and live with one of my parents until the other parent was ready to move East with my brother who was in eighth grade at the time The option which we ended up pursuing was that I would live in a hotel, the Residence Inn, for about two months until we found a house in Boston. My parents took turns staying with me. While I was living in the hotel I found a job during the mornings to do volunteer work at the Massachusetts Eye and Ear Infirmary.

I worked on the children's floor and helped keep the playroom clean and organized. I played with the kids while they waited for surgery or while they waited for their sibling in surgery. One day I had lunch with my coworker, and she saw me taking some pills. She asked what it was, and I told her it was for my mental illness. She didn't respond so I thought she was okay with it.

However, the next day, when I arrived at work, my boss invited me into her office and closed the door.

She asked how come I didn't tell her I have bipolar disorder and that I was a danger to the patients because I could become dangerous anytime and that I shouldn't be working with children. I was not going to let myself be discriminated against. First I told her that she had my diagnosis wrong, I do not have bipolar disorder, I have schizoaffective disorder, and they are different. Then I told her that I take medication and I am not at risk of hurting anyone. I promised that if I felt any kind of weird feeling coming on, I would take a break and ask for help. She wasn't convinced that I was safe to be volunteering and asked me if I would check in with her every morning so she could make sure I was okay. I refused. I told her angrily that no one else had to check in with her and it was not fair to ask me to. I said, "If you're going to treat me differently then I don't want to work here." We sat in silence for three minutes, then she agreed to let me continue working. "But," she said "*never* tell anyone about your disease. Do not tell your coworkers and never mention it in front of the patients." I told her that I would use my common sense.

I guess I should have been more discreet when taking my pills around my coworkers at lunch. I didn't know that my mental illness had to be such a secret. Once I got over the discrimination that I faced, I liked working at the Massachusetts Eye and Ear Infirmary. I could take the T (public transportation) to work, or my dad showed me how to walk from our hotel, across the Charles River, and to the infirmary. I felt independent. My case manager from East House found an evening program for me to join called Two Brattle Center.

I went there weekday evenings from four to eight. There were eight people in our group, and the group lasted for three months. We had three girls and five guys. We had groups like interpersonal group, job/school education, drug group, med group, creative expression, life story, and check-in. From what I hear it is similar to a day program, except the facilities at Two

Brattle were much nicer than the facilities at a hospital. We sat on sofas and cushy chairs while we talked about our issues. The members of the group were all educated young adults. This filled up my evenings and gave me a sense of belonging to the city of Boston. I felt like I had a reason to be there. I had trouble in the groups at first because I would dissociate and lose time and then people would treat me differently. I was the most psychotic one and that could be embarrassing. At Two Brattle I had an administrator, Gabe, and a therapist, Dr. Boor.

Gabe wanted me to fulfill my dreams, but he wanted me to be more independent from my father. He thought my father was controlling too much of my life. The truth was that I needed that support from my father, and without him I would have been lost. Dr. Boor was a great therapist, but not so great for me because I was in love with her. She was beautiful and healthy and perfect. I knew she was out of my realm, but that couldn't stop me from reaching. I didn't tell her right away, but I think she knew.

So I had Dr. Boor and Gabe helping me through my hard times at Two Brattle. I was also seeing Dr. Fluten as my psychiatrist. She had agreed to work with me on a long-term basis after she met me at East House. I had an amazing treatment team yet I was still faltering every now and then.

CHAPTER 7

Denied Again

On May 5, I was admitted to the STU (short-term unit) at McLean Hospital. I was admitted because I was manic. I had started taking an antidepressant (Effexor XR), and it made me violent, angry, agitated, and a bit wild. I hadn't slept in three nights. I paced the Clinical Evaluation Center (CEC), and I talked nonstop. Eventually they put me in a room in the STU. I sat there on the bed, scribbling a letter to no one on the back of the McLean Hospital information sheet. My roommate woke up. She saw me and said, "Hello," and then she went back to sleep. It turned out that my roommate from the CEC in May 1999 would become a close friend whom I still talk to today. Her name is Edie. She had serious difficulties, but they were very different from mine. We got along great. We talked, played Trivial Pursuit, and had matchbox car (which I brought) races down the long hallways. Edie is the best roommate I've ever had. She was also college age, and she was smart and aware of her illness.

Still, I was not hesitant to leave her when I felt calmer and was ready to be discharged. I went back to my volunteer job and my evening program at Two Brattle. I started a kind of therapy, in addition to what I was doing with Dr. Boor, called Dialectical Behavior Therapy (DBT). I had done a little bit of it in East House, and I think it helped me. I worked with Emily, then Cici. I got a manual that I refer back to every now and then for coping techniques. The therapy itself was not too effective because I was very healthy and aware of my behavior and myself. I had a hard time remembering how sick I get sometimes. It is during those very sick times when I need to remember my DBT skills.

Everything was going great for a while. I signed up for summer school at Harvard, an intensive French class. Everything was *en Francais*, and it required at least four hours a day studying French in class, the language lab, and the library. It was fun. I became fluent, and I actually understood movies with no subtitles. The class was hard, but it came easily to me. Halfway through the semester my family moved into our new house in Weston, a suburb of Boston. At first, my dad and I slept on mattresses on the floor with no window shades. My mom would not have approved. Slowly the house developed piece by piece. When my mom and my brother came, we had window coverings, beds, shelves, and drawers for clothes, and we even had palatable tap water. I rode the T (public transportation) into Cambridge every morning for my French class, and then I rode it home in the afternoon.

Every day for lunch I went to Lee's, the best sandwich shop in Cambridge. My real favorite is Subway, but they don't have this chain in Cambridge. Cambridge does have a 7-Eleven though, so I got my fair share of Slurpees, my favorite treat.

As I went to school at Harvard summer school I continued therapy at Two Brattle, even though I wasn't in the program anymore. I still had an issue with the fact that I was in love with my therapist. She was beautiful and smart, and I couldn't stop thinking about her. But, I would be getting a new therapist soon because I was planning on heading to Williams College in the fall of 1999. I had been accepted when I graduated from high school, and I had deferred my admission until this fall. I had been out of the hospital for about six months, I had completed summer school, and I was feeling great. Still, my treatment team (Dr. Fluten, Dr. Boor, and Gabe) had a meeting and decided that I couldn't go. Even though when I talked to them individually they all were optimistic, when they met, they decided that going away to college was a no-go for me.

We had a meeting, and they broke the news to me that I

would not be going away to college and if I wanted to move out
of my house I would have to move into a group home. I was
furious. All I wanted to do was go to college; that had been my
dream for as long as I can remember. They said no. They had no
good reasons, just that they didn't want me to get sick somewhere
without resources to help me. Dr. Fluten told me that she was
not comfortable being my doctor when she was so far away from
me. At least I got an honest answer from her. The rest of them
just said they didn't think I was ready. For an entire week I cried
and was miserable. The day when I was supposed to leave came
and went. I watched my older brother Ben go away to college.
He told me that I wasn't missing much. Still, I wanted to be a
college student. I signed up for a writing class at Harvard Extension
School. But, that didn't start until the end of September.

Weird things started happening in my life. I would be at
home in bed, and then I would blink, and I would be at the
video store. I wouldn't know how I got there, and I would have
to search around the area for my car and my car keys. It happened
often when I was walking, then I would blink, and I would be
somewhere else. Sometimes hours passed, sometimes just
minutes. This "losing time" had happened before when I was
younger, but it never happened this frequently in such a short
time frame. Then I started waking up during the night only to
find myself in the bathroom covered with blood. Or I would
blink and find myself in a public bathroom with razor cuts all
over me, and I wouldn't know where I got the razor. I could tell
it was a razor cut because of the two parallel lines. I told Dr.
Fluten about this, and she was concerned. Then I went to see
Cici, my DBT therapist, and she saw what I had done to myself
without even remembering one incident and called Dr. Fluten.
We all agreed that I should be in the hospital.

After sitting in the CEC for four hours I got to speak with a
doctor. This was where I met Dr. Yamon. She was the resident
doctor who was doing my intake, and she assigned me to NB1,
the floor where she works. I refused to go to NB2 because I
thought the doctors there were in a conspiracy to kill me. I got

transferred to NB1, and I was "coming and going" the whole time. I would be talking to a nurse, and then all of a sudden I would not know what she was talking about. Nevertheless, the doctors, nurses, and staff all seemed very nice. No one knew what was causing my losing-time episodes, and no one even knew what they were. The second day there I cut myself with a pen cap without realizing it. I just blinked, and my arm was bloody, and I had part of a pen cap in my hand. Most of the time I was perfectly healthy, so it was kind of weird to be in the hospital. I saw my doctor, Dr. Ivanho, every day, and he communicated with Dr. Fluten for me. Dr. Fluten came to visit me frequently, and she would explain to me what was going on and would tell me what she thought was happening to me. When I was well, I had long talks with Dr. Yamon, the resident on my treatment team We would sit outside and talk about my life and when I had lost time in the past and what triggered it. We came up with some meaningful patterns but nothing to stop the episodes. I didn't remember what happened when I lost time, but the staff told me that I was just real quiet and suspicious. They said I failed to recognize people whom I would know when I got out of the episode. One doctor even told me that I forgot how to tell time. One theory was that the antipsychotic meds I was on were not working well enough. Dr. Fluten suggested trying me on clozapine, the med for those who are treatment resistant.

Clozapine is also the most "serious" drug to me; it has terrible side effects, and blood has to be drawn every week at first. This would prevent me from traveling, which I did not want to give up. Anyway, I had to get a normal EEG before I could try clozapine. My EEG came back with some sort of abnormal spikes which meant that I couldn't take clozapine because it lowers the seizure threshold. With this new information, my treatment team decided that I needed a seventy-two-hour EEG to check if the losing-time episodes I was having were some sort of temporal lobe seizures.

The seventy-two-hour EEG was unlike anything I've ever experienced before. My dad had to get special permission to take

me out of the hospital when I was only on level 1 (most hospitals
I've been to have the same level system). We went to the office,
and the technician glued about thirty electrodes to my head. The
glue he used smelled like rubber cement. Then he wrapped my
head up like a mummy to help the electrodes stay in place. I had
a waistband with a panic button for me to press in case I felt
something happening. I also had a big box that had to be plugged
into the wall wherever I went. Everyone looked at me funny
when I got back to the unit. I went to my bed to rest. My dad
brought in my nurse and my staff person and showed them how
the panic button works and how to plug in the box. They had to
know in case my dad wasn't there and I got confused about how
it worked. I had to keep the same shirt on for seventy-two hours.

The first time I started feeling confused about where I was
and what was going on, I remembered to press the panic button
Everyone was as helpful as possible to accommodate my box and
me. A few patients asked if the surgery hurt, and I had to tell
them it was just an EEG. The second time I don't remember, but
Dr. Yamon told me that she came into my room, and I didn't
recognize her and was very confused and suspicious of everyone.
She asked the nurse to press the panic button, but I was lying on
my side, and the button was around my waist, and I freaked out
when she tried to press it. I don't know if she ended up pressing
it or not, I don't remember. Finally the day came to take off the
head wrap. One of the staff, Emma, got out the comb and the
solution they gave me, and we pulled off the electrodes one by
one. It took about an hour to get them all off. Once, I touched
my eye and got the solution in my eye, and it hurt worse than a
bee sting. We ran to the bathroom and flushed my eye with
water until it felt better. Eventually they were all off, and I took
a shower to rinse the rest of the sticky stuff off. One shower
didn't do it though; that glue was on my head for days. I thanked
Emma a million times because she had helped me get them off;
I don't think I could have done it by myself.

I was in the hospital for six weeks so I became friends with
some of the younger staff. They played games with me and talked

to me. They kept me amused. In particular there was one staff person whom I got along great with, Kaitlin. She would come in my room during the day and just sit and talk to me until someone needed her help. She made me feel like a normal person, even though I was a psychiatric patient who was so sick that no one knew what was wrong with me or how to help me.

I did feel rather desperate. I wanted to know what was wrong with me so I could get some help. The results of the seventy-two-hour EEG came back normal. Dr. Fluten wasn't convinced that I didn't have a seizure disorder though. She thought there could be seizures that don't show up on EEGs. There was a meeting between my treatment team and some knowledgeable people from around the hospital. In addition to a team of psychiatric workers, there were a few neurologists there. I met with each doctor individually before they met as a team. One of the more experienced older doctors told me that I had schizophrenia, and I was only going to deteriorate in the next few years, and I should give up my hopes of going to college. Another doctor told me that all my problems came from my family, and I needed to move out as soon as possible, preferably into a group home. Dr. Boor maintained that I could get through anything with time and medication. Dr. Fluten wanted to try me on Tegretol, an anticonvulsant.

So we tried Tegretol, and it worked! On Tegretol I did not have any lost-time episodes, and I felt great, just a little tired. At that point we did not know why Tegretol worked, but I was desperate to get out of the hospital and start that writing class that I had signed up for, so I got discharged. They suggested that I move into a group home on the McLean campus, but I wanted to go home.

The doctors were afraid that my dad was pressuring me to come home and that after a five-week hospital stay I needed a transition where I could be watched more closely. It is true that my dad influenced my decision; he told me that he could take care of me at home. With my mom and dad taking care of me 24/7, there was no reason for me to go to a group home.

Before I could be discharged from the hospital I had to see a neurologist one more time. This time they wanted me to see a *child* neurologist. The child neurologist examined me thoroughly, doing all the normal neurological tests (touch your fingers, walk in a straight line, push with both hands) and other tests. Then she examined my body, even the parts that I did not want to be examined. She came up with a few things, and she ordered blood tests. I had to wake up early and eat three waffles before one test. I followed her directions, but I thought the child neurologist did not find anything by doing her weird tests. Prior to discharge I also had to see a psychologist for extensive neuropsychological testing. I made an appointment for the testing after my discharge. Then I saw my neurologist again, not the child neurologist but the doctor whom I had initially seen. He thought that I should see a neuroendocrinologist. He thought this was needed to rule out a disorder which is prevalent among Ashkenazi Jewish people like myself. It is called Late Onset Congenital Adrenal Hyperplasia or LOCAH.

The neuroendocrinologist first interviewed me and then did the usual neurological tests. He also took a blood sample. When that blood sample came back positive for some type of androgen, he ordered a two-hour cortrosyn stimulation test. My dad took me to the lab, and I sat in a recliner with an IV in my arm. Every thirty minutes the nurse put something into the IV. I still have no idea how the test works, but my level (of whatever they were testing) came back high. I was diagnosed with LOCAH. I know everything about all of my medical issues, except the LOCAH. I do not fully understand how it works, and I am convinced that I don't really have it. He said that if I took meds it would help with my acne, but I think my acne comes from taking lithium, not having LOCAH. Maybe meds could help me lose weight— but I think my weight inflations came from eating too much because Zyprexa made me hungry. I don't have any of the other symptoms like too much body hair, hair thinning on the head, sporadic periods, and who knows what else. Since my diagnosis, my parents have both been diagnosed with LOCAH in the same lab. I think the lab is fixed. That is how I rationalize my high test results with the fact that I don't think I have it. But, going along with this doctor whom I do trust, I decided to try a steroid medication, Cortef.

There were supposed to be no side effects. Cortef made me psychotic, and I was hospitalized. The psychosis was all centered around Dr. Boor, my therapist with whom I was in love. I wanted to kill her. I had it all worked out, I ordered the gun online, and then in my ranting and ravings I forgot that if I told anyone they would send me away. So I went to see my DBT therapist, and I told her, and you can figure out what happened from there. I ended up back on NB1. This was right before Christmas of 1999. I was only there for about a week, and then once I was off the Cortef everything seemed fine.

The issue remained though of how I was going to go to therapy with a therapist whom I had had full intentions of raping and murdering only one week ago. I decided to be open, and I told Dr. Boor that I was in love with her, and I couldn't carry on with her as my therapist. She wanted to talk about it and get some closure. She didn't understand just how hard it was for me to sit in a room alone with her.

I had Dr. Yamon in the back of my mind. She was my resident doctor whom I had gotten along so well with when I was an inpatient in NB1. She had told me that she had a therapy slot open. I called her. She still had a slot open so Dr. Yamon became my therapist.

One of the nights when I was still seeing Dr. Boor, and I had already told her about my feelings, I had an emergency. I was suicidal. I couldn't go to bed because I was going to kill myself. After trying to distract myself for a couple hours I paged Cici. I could not page Dr. Boor, and I figured it was kind of a therapy issue, plus I had seen her earlier that day, and she knew this might happen. I rarely page my doctors, but this was a true emergency. She called back and talked me into bed. She told me that if I woke up at any point or if I couldn't sleep for more than thirty minutes, I should call her. She gave me her home telephone number.

Sure enough the sleeping pill knocked me out, and I woke up at 8:00 a.m. full of fear. I was afraid to get out of bed because I thought I might go downstairs and kill myself. I paged Cici. I told her that I was really feeling bad, and I couldn't get out of bed, and I wanted to call Dr. Fluten, the head of my treatment team. She said that I should absolutely not call Dr. Fluten and that she was going to call me back in ten minutes.

"Brooke, I have called the police; they will be at your house in twenty minutes." That's what Cici told me when she called back. I was furious. I told her that my mom would come home and take care of me if I called her, and most importantly she said that I couldn't call Dr. Fluten until I arrived at the hospital. Cici called my mom at the beauty salon, and she came home fast enough to cancel the police. And then the phone rang; it was Dr. Fluten. "Why didn't you call me?" she asked. I told her that Cici said I couldn't. The situation got out of hand, and with all the commotion I was feeling even more suicidal. Dr. Fluten saw me at two o'clock that afternoon, and we talked at length about how suicide is not an option. When I told her about the police, she said that they came because Dr. Boor signed the pink paper (aka the involuntary commitment sheet). When I asked her why she signed it she said that Cici told her I was in bed with a knife ready to kill myself. They called it a miscommunication. I say either Cici lied or Dr. Boor lied. Their "miscommunication" nearly cost me a stay in the hospital and a ride in the police car. I knew that I could not work with people like that anymore.

Fortunately I had found Dr. Yamon for therapy. I decided to try some CBT (cognitive behavior therapy) instead of DBT, and I got some names from Dr. Fluten. I wanted my whole treatment team to be at McLean. I also wanted people with whom I could work without having to worry about someone lying. I found Dr. Samy through Dr. Fluten's recommendation. Dr. Samy and I began to work on CBT techniques and methods to fight my thought disorder.

In the midst of all this excitement I had to follow up on the promise I made to have neuropsychological testing done. I think the neurologist had ordered the testing to make sure that he wasn't missing any problems with my brain. The tests took eight hours over three days. I refused to take the Rorschach test, but other than that I complied. The Rorschach frustrated me because I never saw anything besides blobs of ink. I had already done it twice, and I didn't want to do it again. I was medicated and tired, so I was not sure how accurate those tests were. Nevertheless, I completed all my assignments and was home from my second fall 1999 hospital stay just in time for the New Year.

CHAPTER 8

The Big Orange Pill

Sparkling cider and a seat on the sofa with my dog at my feet. The millennium was a blast. I had few friends; most of them from high school were in Seattle. I watched the New Year begin all over the world. There were fireworks, dancers, concerts, and lots of people. Watching the celebrations made me realize my life was boring, but that was the way I wanted it. I had had enough excitement in the fall to last me a while. I was lonely though.

I wanted to go to school, more than just night school. There were a few colleges around where we lived, and Brandeis University offered a "Special Students Program" for people to attend and take courses without working towards a degree. I applied and was accepted for the spring 2000. Finally my life was going somewhere.

My parents and doctors told me that the only thing I could do to mess up my life would be to take drugs and alcohol. I also saw how much drugs and alcohol messed people up in the hospitals and RTCs I had been in. I couldn't help myself though. Everyone I knew drank. I had a few friends from the program in Cambridge at Two Brattle Center. They were all at least twenty-one, so it wasn't illegal for them to drink. I was lonely, and when my friend Samantha called and asked if I wanted to come over for a Super Bowl party, I said yes. I knew there would be drinking and drugs there. I thought I would be able to sustain the peer pressure. But when I saw everyone else drinking, I couldn't help myself I had two shots of Absolute vodka. They burned as they went down. My mom came to give me a ride home, and she did not even notice I had had a few drinks. We got home late, and I tried to go to sleep. I felt so guilty because I knew alcohol was bad for me. In the back of my mind, I also wondered how much I could drink without becoming psychotic. I started thinking about drinking some of the beer or wine that my parents kept in the house. I was so scared that my thinking was going in the wrong direction. I called Dr. Fluten even though it was one o'clock in the morning. Dr. Fluten understood and told me it was okay, and I should just go to sleep.

Drinking certainly put my life on hold. My parents let my doctor talk to me about it first. She was not mean, but she was not happy. Then we had a family meeting. The basic consensus was that since everyone in my life is working so hard to make my life better, I either needed to join the bandwagon, or move out of the house and find my own way. They were not going to help me if I was going to go and screw everything up. One surefire way for a mentally ill person to mess up their life is to drink alcohol or use drugs.

Dr. Fluten and my parents were not going to let that happen. So we made a contract.

CONTRACT

If I: 1) feel suicidal
        2) feel like cutting myself
        3) feel like misusing my medication
        4) hear voices
        5) get confused thoughts so I'm not thinking clearly

I Will: 1) call Dr. B . . .
        2) call G . . .
        3) call Dr. F . . .

If it is an emergency where I have a suicidal plan or a plan to hurt myself *I will*

1) page G . . .
2) page Dr.F . . .

If it is an emergency I will tell my mom or dad and go to the Emergency Room.

I will attend the program every weekday evening and I will participate and not leave without telling staff where I am going.

Things I discuss with Dr.B . . . In therapy will be kept confidential between me and her unless she is concerned about my safety, and except when she is endeavoring to keep the treatment team informed of pastimes and useful clinical information.

If any staff feels the need to communicate with my parents about me and my safety they will tell me before they call my parents so I get warned of the situation, if it is possible to do so.

Actually I made the contract, but we all had to sign it. I like living on a contract; it makes me feel like I am in control of my destiny because everything is predictable. One thing I remember about growing up was feeling that my parents' reactions were unpredictable. One time I got screamed at for coming home five minutes late for dinner. But, another time I got caught coming home two hours past curfew, and my parents weren't even angry. It was unpredictable.

In the spring I started as a student at Brandeis. I woke up at 9 a.m., and my parents had to drive me to school because my driver's license had been revoked. This is something my parents did when I was hospitalized in December. School was mostly very boring. Mondays and Thursdays I went to Psychology 1A. The professor used many demonstrations, and the class was generally interesting. I always sat in the front row with its comfortable chairs so I could be more relaxed, yet I would feel guilty when I fell asleep because I was in the front. I was still on a lot of meds (lithium, Tegretol, Zyprexa, Moban, Cogentin), and it took a big effort for me not to fall asleep during a lecture. Monday, Wednesday, and Friday I had Physics 9B, which is basic physics. I had the same problem with wanting to fall asleep, but I knew that I would miss information that would be on the exam. Finally, I had calculus. I love math, and calculus was fun and challenging. I had already had calculus in high school, but I didn't remember most of it. I really don't remember most of high school. I remember soccer practices and games and conversations I had with teachers, but I don't remember what books or movies that I read or watched in high school are about. I can walk around a bookstore and point to all the books that I know I've read, but I don't remember what they were about.

The spring term was fun, and it was a good way to get me integrated into life with people my age. But I didn't integrate as well as I thought I would. It seemed as though one would have to live on campus in order to really be a part of campus life and make friends. I wanted to join the lacrosse team, but I didn't know how or if I was allowed to because I was a special student. I spent most of my time with my mom and dad. I managed to stay out of the hospital for the entire spring semester. I made a goal to stay out of the hospital for all of the year 2000. I'm into making attainable goals, and I figured this would be perfect.

I believed at the time and I sort of believe now that I was so sick because I was a bad child. I can't come up with any other reason why I might have been psychotic, and things just don't happen without a reason. I don't know what I did that was bad, and that is what I'm trying to figure out now. Some people say that there are no bad children, just children who do bad things. I disagree. I was a bad child. But, I do believe that I overcame that. I was healthy, and I thought that I was never going to get sick again.

I signed up for Brandeis summer school. The two courses that interested me were "Sexuality and Cinema" and "Families." I signed up to be a residential student. I was going to live on campus! Assuming that everything went well on my family's trip to Europe, I had convinced Dr. Fluten and my parents that it was a good idea for me to live on campus as a transition to living there in the fall. Over the summer I could have a single room, and I could see if I liked it. I talked to the head of the Brandeis Psychological Counseling Center, and he recommended that I live at home over the summer because the campus was dead and there was nothing to do and no one to talk to. But I had my eyes set on living in a single room on campus during the summer. The reason I was so adamant was because I was so lonely; I wanted friends. But, I did not make any. The campus was dead. I had four suitemates, and I rarely saw them. I ate by myself and spent my time reading in my room. I was even lonelier because I didn't have my parents to talk to.

My classes were challenging, but after a week I had to drop out of the Sexuality and Cinema class. I was having violent sexual thoughts, and Dr. Fluten decided that seeing movies about sexuality might trigger more violent sexual thoughts. When I say that I was having those thoughts, it was not just like a little thought in my head, the thoughts came into my head and took over, and they were disgusting and violent and often involved me doing something to someone else, which made me feel guilty and confused. So, I was just taking one class, and I was bored at school. I moved back home. I kept my stuff at school, and I went back every now and then, but I mostly lived at home.

I don't even want to get into it because it is so stupid, but Brandeis couldn't give me a single room for the fall, even though I had a medical reason. They had no rooms. They admitted too many students and had nowhere to house them. So I was going to spend the fall living at home, and if I felt okay, I could move into the dorms for second semester in January.

I drove my red Volvo, which I could now legally drive, the three miles to Brandeis, and I parked in the T-lot way down the hill. I thought that's where commuters had to park. First stop: office of public safety. They sold me a parking pass and told me to park in the T-lot. Score. Next stop: office where they give out student ID cards. I smiled for the picture and waited two minutes for the lamination to dry. Then I headed to my first class. Chemistry was in the big lecture hall in the science building; there must have been about 150 people in the room. The professor seemed strict and very organized. She handed out a syllabus and directed us towards the chemistry website to see what we were supposed to read by when.

I sat off to the right and observed the room. Most people were nervous; chemistry had a reputation of being hard. I like science though, so I wasn't too nervous. My lab was scheduled for Friday, and it didn't start for a couple of weeks. Next I headed off to my USEM (University Seminar) on Science and Western Society. The professor was a nice guy, but the class had a bad combination of quiet students and a professor who was content to hear himself talk for fifty minutes. It was a very different type of class; there was no syllabus or handouts. We read books and then discussed them without taking notes because the two short papers that we wrote were completely on our opinion, not facts or evidence from the books. On the first day we mostly just talked about school logistical issues of how to get places and how to do things like use the telephone. I had an hour for lunch, and then I had swimming class.

"You know how to swim?" asked the coach.

"I think so," I replied, "just not real well." Everyone in the class was on a different level. I have always wanted to know how to swim properly, so I loved the feedback I got. Being in the pool gave me a chance to loosen up some muscles and get a little exercise. I love to swim. I struggled to find bathing suits that fit comfortably, but I compromised with some.

On Thursday afternoon I had my favorite class, UWS (University Writing Seminar). The class actually was pretty bad most of the time; it was the writing assignments that I liked. The class often had long conversations about grammar, which were boring. Three times we got to hear our classmates' writing read out loud, and that was enjoyable. I wish we had done more peer editing like we started out doing. The assignments were challenging though. We got to write editorials, nonfiction essays, and analysis papers about the short stories we read. My favorite paper was the paper I wrote "On pockets . . ." I tested myself to see if I could fill three pages on pockets, and it turned out to be fun. School was going well until I got obsessive thoughts again.

I developed shower rituals about the order of washing and rinsing. I had to get dressed in a certain order and at a certain pace. I had to take my pills in a certain order, and if I messed that up, I had to punish myself with getting dressed even faster. Once the rule was broken, there was pretty much no way for me to fix it; it just meant that I was going to die. I always have certain orders and rituals for life, but they never interfered with my life until now. I told my therapist about this, and he recommended that I read a book about obsessive-compulsive disorder. With the book he suggested I start slowly but attempt to break one ritual. So, I decided to wash my hair before my body. It was a disaster. I couldn't stop worrying about dying. I felt like I was having a panic attack and the only way I could get over it would be to take another shower and do it in the right order. I tried taking another shower, and I still felt scared and panicky, so I paged my therapist who had told me to do this. I figured he was trying to kill me, and I wanted to get in a few words to him before I died. No response. I paged my psychiatrist to see if she had any ideas. No response. Finally I paged my therapist at a different hospital, and she called back. She helped me calm down enough so that I could just take a sleeping pill and go to sleep. I felt okay the next morning; the rituals were back to normal. I was coping.

Then, the thoughts got violent. I would be sitting in class, and I would see a beautiful girl. It only took one glance to get her into my head. Once she was in my head, she was mine. She was blonde with a firm, tight body, just like the rest of them. My thoughts were words, and I carried on a conversation with my girl. Her voice turned me on, and I was stuck in class. I couldn't tell the difference between what I was really doing and what I was just doing in my head. I raped her, and then I murdered her. After she was dead I would realize that I hadn't caused enough pain or blood so I would start over and do it again. I thought I was over the blood thing ever since I stopped cutting myself, but now I found the blood arousing again. I wrote it down in detail and showed it to Dr. Samy, my therapist. Then I showed it to Dr. Yamon, and finally the word got around to Dr. Fluten that I was having some trouble. She was frustrated that she did not hear sooner. Without hesitation she wanted me in the hospital. She said it was unsafe for someone in my state to be out on my own, even if my parents were watching me. My parents were there, and they were confused. I told them everything about my thoughts, even the details about the rapes and the murders. My parents and Dr. Fluten walked me over to the CEC to be admitted to the hospital.

In the CEC the staff took my blood pressure, temperature, and weight. They asked me to agree to an evaluation. They searched my bag. I didn't know of any blades in my bag, and they didn't find any. Then the waiting game began. One hour passed, a nurse came to take my blood sugar. My diabetes has been inactive for two years, but I guess they just wanted to be thorough. Two hours passed, I talked to a girl who had never been in the hospital before. Three hours passed, the nurse came to interview me about my history and medications. I don't remember anything more than the girls inside my head. I had to keep it inside my head. Four hours passed, the doctor came and interviewed me to see if I should be admitted. She was impatient and frustrated with my wandering thoughts. She didn't understand that someone else was in control of my brain. They asked me to sign myself into the hospital. I did. Five hours passed; my doctor from the last two hospitalizations came to see me.

I respected Dr. Ivanho. He is smart, and he always listened to me, which was rare. He took me into a conference room in the CEC and asked me what restrictions and privileges I wanted. I was near tears from the whole ordeal, and seeing a familiar face made me feel much better. He knew that I wasn't a bad person even though all I could think about was the girls whom I wanted to murder.

Dr. Ivanho got me admitted to NB1, and I moved over there at about 8:00 at night. My room was the quiet room because that was the only single room available. I requested a single room because I was afraid that I might hurt my roommate. None of the staff really believed me that there was anything wrong because I didn't talk about it, it was just my thoughts that were out of control. The staff cleaned my room with Listerine because they found that it kills odor better than Lysol. They took away all my clothes and stuff. I didn't really bring much, still I assumed they would give it back after they inspected it. But that's not how it worked. They told me that the doctor's orders were to keep me locked in the quiet room all alone with nothing but a hospital gown to cover me. I was supposed to eat in the quiet room too, so when my parents showed up for dinner, they immediately called Dr. Ivanho and had him change the orders. It was just a miscommunication, but I am glad my parents came to take care of me.

Every distraction I could get was great. I sat out in the common room, looking at men, trying to get the women out of my head. It didn't work. I sat in my room, trying to concentrate on the schoolwork I was missing, but I couldn't concentrate well at all. I started to get off of Zyprexa, one of my meds which was possibly contributing to my obsessive thoughts. I was only on a small dose, and it wasn't helping me at all. After a few days, once I was off Zyprexa, I started a new med, an antipsychotic called Mellaril.

It was a big orange pill. I'm not sure how Dr. Fluten chose Mellaril, but everything I had heard about it was that it was old and dangerous. I had read in drug books that Mellaril is rarely used anymore because it has been replaced by the newer meds. Still, I was up for a try. The newer drugs hadn't worked too well for me. We increased the dose pretty fast, wanting to get me out of the hospital and back in school. At 300 mg we stopped. I was bored in the hospital. One can only watch so much daytime TV. I refused to go to the groups because I had already been to them all during previous stays, and they are all designed for low-functioning people. So at 300 mg of Mellaril in addition to all my other meds, I was feeling great, and I wanted to be discharged.

The doctors all agreed that I was doing well, and I should go home and get some blood tests and an EKG done. I went back to school and back to lacrosse practice. I found that in chemistry I had missed a lot, and it was hard for me to understand what was going on because I had missed the foundation. In everything else I was fine. I felt good to be back at school and with my lacrosse team. A couple days later I drove down to MGH and got my blood work and EKG done.

The next day I was at lacrosse practice after school. When I got home my mom told me that I had to page Dr. Fluten immediately because there was something wrong on my EKG. I called Dr. Fluten, and she said that my QT interval was elongated. I didn't know what that meant, but later she told me that it was very dangerous. At the time, she told me not to exercise and then we went through a whole series of lowering the Mellaril so that it was still effective, yet monitoring my EKG so that my heart was normal. We finally ended up with a QT interval slightly elevated and the Mellaril at 150 mg. I had to go to a cardiologist to get an examination, an "echo cardio-something" and a stress test. I had to ride a bike with no sports bra on for ten minutes. Fortunately these tests all came back normal so my heart was in fine condition.

So, anyway, I missed all of the lacrosse season with my heart issues, and that was sad because I love sports. I didn't miss any more school though. I dropped out of chemistry at the last moment because I thought I was going to fail. But, I finished my first semester as an undergrad student at Brandeis successfully.

I had no final exams which was lucky. I felt kind of stupid because I was only able to pass two and one-half courses while most people took four. Still I just tried to remember that I was in no rush to complete college. My primary worry was to stay healthy. I joined a weight-loss program at McLean Hospital called TRIAD. It involved exercising and eating proteins for lunch and carbs for dinner. Plus, there was a drink that I took before lunch and dinner. It didn't taste too bad if I mixed it with seltzer.

Over break I traveled with my family to Hawaii and Colorado. My weight had come down so much that I was able to out-ski my dad. The last time we went skiing I could barely make it down the mountain. Finally I went back to school. I was taking Calculus 2, Biology: Paradigms of Biological Investigation, and Psychology: Learning and Behavior. Lacrosse started back up again, and we practiced in the gym in the evenings. And then my grandma became very ill. She was diagnosed with lung cancer in August, and she had surgery. The surgeon told her the cancer was all gone. It came back. She saw an oncologist who said she needed chemotherapy, but before she could even start chemotherapy, the cancer had spread throughout her body, and she was too weak to get any treatment. She died on February 10, 2001. I saw her in the hospital about ten days before she died, and she was very sick. I walked in the hospital room and looked around. I didn't even recognize her at first. At least I got to say goodbye in my own way.

I went back to school, and I had my midterms. I failed. It wasn't just like I did poorly, I really failed. I began working then to decide what I wanted to do. I could take a leave of absence from school, I could drop one class and focus on the other two, I could drop out of school altogether, or I could keep my schedule as it was and just keep trying. I was not sure what to do. I still had no friends except those people whom I saw in class or at lacrosse. I was lonely. I am not stupid, and there was no reason why I should have been failing. My doctor and my parents kept telling me I am too hard on myself. I needed to give myself credit for trying and for coming as far as I have. I reached out to a girl on my lacrosse team and told her that I have schizoaffective disorder. She was surprised, but she was very nice. I wondered what it would be like if everyone knew. I hate having to keep myself a secret. I hate to let the stigma hold me back.

CHAPTER 9

I Think I Scared Her

I found myself in the quiet room once again. The floor still smelled like Listerine, and the bed was still on the ground. The Mellaril was not the right med for me because when I got it at a low-enough dose so that it was safe for my heart, it did not control my psychosis. The plan was to take a break from everything: school, lacrosse, weight loss, travel, E-mails, and anything else I could worry about. I was going to switch to a brand-new medication called Geodon which just became available in the United States.

I couldn't go on Geodon and Mellaril at the same time because of the heart risks so I had to get completely off one before I could start the other. During the week, when I was switching, I had some of the worst psychosis that I had ever experienced. Tears constantly flowed from my eyes. I talked in a confused language that no one understood. People's faces manipulated themselves when I looked at them. The voices, which I hadn't heard in months, started screaming and commanding again. It was terrible for me and my family. I think it was probably also pretty bad for the staff and doctors. People stared at me. I hadn't showered because I wasn't allowed to take a shower alone, and I refused to let the staff watch me shower. I had on the same clothes that I slept in because there was nowhere for me to change into the clean clothes that my parents brought me. If I tried to change in the quiet room, people could just look in the window. I was terrified of having someone see me without my shirt on.

Everywhere I went people were staring at me. I sat in the quiet room with the door open, and then I wandered down the hall because I was bored.

I accused everyone who looked at me twice of staring and trying to see into my eyes. After four nights I moved into a regular room; it was a single room though because I was still having thoughts about killing people. There was a blond woman on the staff who had long hair and brilliant blue eyes. She was short and thin, yet she looked strong. She looked substantial. I followed her around the unit. I stared at her with all my might because in my head I was murdering her. Over and over again. When she went into the back staff room behind the office, I sat by the office windows and waited for her to come out. All day I shadowed her. Finally she asked me to stop, and I told her I was going to kill her. I think I scared her. I didn't mean to scare her; I was only telling her the truth. She told my staff contact, and we had a talk about how I was not going to kill anyone, it was all in my head, and I was able to go to sleep that night with just a little extra Ativan. That MHS whom I wanted to kill never came back to my unit (NB1) for the rest of the time that I was there.

Before I got hospitalized I knew something was wrong. I met with Dr. Yamon, my therapist, as usual, on Friday morning at ten o'clock, but this time it was different. All I could think about was killing. I was staring at Dr. Yamon so intently that it made her uncomfortable enough to ask me what was going on. I told her I was going to kill. She said that I seemed angry and tried to ask me what I was angry about. "I'm going to kill you."

Then I left. I got in my car and drove to my school and walked around trying to plan the best route for me to follow when I was going to go on my shooting spree. I was not thinking anything through, just following the voices. *"Kill him, kill her, kill them all . . ."*

When I got home I called Dr. Fluten, and an emergency meeting was scheduled. I simply told her how I was going to kill Dr. Yamon, and I was going to go on a killing spree and kill as many people as possible. I was going to do this not because I hated any of them, but because I needed to kill. Dr. Fluten walked me and my parents over to the CEC. The decision of whether to try a new med had been made for us because my psychosis was breaking through the low level of Mellaril. But, I did not know I was psychotic. I was invigorated to kill.

The pink rubbery chairs stuck to my legs so I didn't sit down. I paced the CEC, waiting for them to admit me to the hospital. Supposedly the CEC is the evaluation center, but for me that night I knew that I was going to end up in the hospital, and I just hoped that I could go to NB1 where I knew all the nurses, and Dr. Ivanho could be my doctor.

Dr. Ivanho is one of the best doctors ever. Every time I go in the hospital I want him to be my doctor because I know that he really cares about me (or else he's a good pretender). Before I met him, when I was hospitalized, the other doctors would just change all my meds and not listen to me. All they wanted was for me to get discharged. But Dr. Ivanho really helped me get better.

The Geodon gave me insomnia at first so I stayed up until 2 a.m. and then woke up at 5 a.m. I felt great. I made friends with the night staff, and I read a lot of books.

People tell me that it's amazing how I can be so extremely sick and psychotic and then in just one week I can be feeling energetic and positive. I don't know why this happens, but maybe it's because I want to get better so badly.

Things are back to normal with Dr. Yamon now, but it took some adjusting. I scared her I think. I scared myself. Killing is permanent, and if I had killed someone, I would have spent the rest of my life in prison. I would have had it on my mind that I ended someone's life and I ruined someone's family. Dr. Yamon and I talked when I was in the hospital about how important it is to be honest and to ask for help when I need it.

About one week before I was admitted to the hospital I called my friend Kalie who has been living with cancer since high school. For about fifteen minutes we talked about school, the weather, and other friends. She did not mention to me that she was dying. The Wednesday after I was discharged I got an E-mail from Vi,

Kalie's sister. Kalie had passed away. My friend and fellow sufferer since high school was gone. I hadn't seen her for a year, and I didn't have a chance to say goodbye. I was devastated.

Kalie was such a fighter. I never saw someone fight so hard. Cancer is a terrible illness. It took my grandma's life and now Kalie's. I had lost two friends in the past to suicide, but that was different. It was different because when I lost those two other friends, I was so immature. I was numb. I didn't feel anything. When I heard about Kalie's death, I was sad. She was not my best friend, but I respected her a lot, and I felt she respected me. We were friends.

I called Dr. Yamon. "My friend died."

"Brooke, I'm so sorry. What happened?"

I explained about the cancer, and Dr. Yamon remembered me talking about Kalie in the past. I couldn't cry. Maybe I was angry. I felt sort of angry. How was one supposed to feel when a friend dies? After ten minutes of me saying nothing and Dr. Yamon not helping at all, I hung up. I wasn't ready to talk.

That night I called Dr. Fluten. When she answered the phone I started to cry. It was the first time I had ever felt sad, at least, that I could remember. I cried and cried. I told her I could feel it inside me. I told her about my pact with Kalie that we made when we were both in the hospital in high school We promised that we were both going to beat our illnesses. Kalie treated me like my illness was just as real as hers. She was one of the few, as most people treated me as if I was faking my illness. So we had this pact, and now Kalie was dead. I was going to have to carry it out myself. I told Dr. Fluten that I felt lonely. I felt pain. I felt so many things! I decided not to go to Kalie's celebration of life in Seattle; I would honor her in my own way. The weekend after she died I wrote her a long letter. I sat in the corner of the library and wrote, listening to the Indigo Girls. I cried all by myself. And then I moved on. For several weeks I felt a pain inside my heart. Then it slowly faded. In no way have I forgotten how special Kalie was and in no way has her determination ceased to impress me. However, I had to move on. I wanted to talk to her friends, her close friends. But I didn't know how, I didn't know what to say. I thought about them a lot because they were my friends too. *I'm going to call someday.*

So I was out of the hospital. I had missed ten days of school. I was enrolled in three classes: math, bioscience, and psychology. I was failing math and psychology because I had missed so much time. I wanted to drop those two classes and keep bioscience, but that meant a trip to the dean's office. The last time I had approached the dean, I had felt intimidated by her, as she had treated me like a "bad student" rather than a student with special needs. However, I needed her help in getting through the present rough time, not her crap about the school rules and how they were unbendable. But, I had no choice but to go back to the dean.

"Hi, I don't know if you remember me, but I met you earlier this semester. I have been in the hospital for ten days, and I'm not going to pass two of my classes. I have a medical excuse, and I'm looking to drop all of my classes except one."

The dean suggested that I take a leave of absence from school and that I drop all my classes and take some time off. I wanted credit for the one class that I could complete. I wrote a petition to the school (it was actually to some board, but I forgot the name). I explained that I had a 3.7 GPA in all the classes I have completed. I'm not a bad student; it's just that my health got in the way this semester. Why wouldn't they let me take the credit for the one class that I was able to complete?

Well, my petition passed, and I earned an A in my one class. Now, adding up all the work that I've done in community college and summer school, I'm going into the fall semester as a sophomore with equal standing to all other sophomores. They tell me I have to take a full-course load. I tell them I'm only going to take a three-quarter-course load. They tell me I'm not going to graduate. I tell them that I will graduate. I'm thinking of transferring schools because I don't like the way I am treated. I'm going to give Brandeis one more semester to see if I like it any better. And, if not, then I'm going to transfer.

On my next semester at Brandeis I'm not going to be so reserved. I'm going to announce my disability to the school. "I have schizoaffective disorder, and I need accommodations!" I'm going to ask for extended test periods if I need it. I'm going to ask for support in making friends and keeping them without them getting scared of me. There must be other students in similar situations, and I'm going to find them. It's not just my illness that I have been protecting at Brandeis, I'm not going to be embarrassed to hold the hand of a girl whom I like or to tell people that I live at home with my family if I still do.

And if I still do live with my family, that will be fine. I'm going to decide during the summer if I want to live in an independent living house (kind of like a group home), the dorms, or at home. I'm going to take my time becoming independent, there's no rush. I got all stressed out last week because I was feeling scared and overwhelmed. I was getting better and growing up, and it was too much all at once. I was trying to get a job, thinking about full-time school, thinking about moving out, taking care of myself, and I became suicidal. I made myself sick in a way. I did too much. I cut myself after not cutting in three years.

I stood in the shower, contemplating life and death—how was I going to kill myself? Without even thinking I took the blade to the inside of my leg and pressed hard. I made three quick cuts. I always cut in threes. *Why did I just do that? That felt good.* And then I sat down in the tub and just let the water bounce off the top of my head.

I called Dr. Yamon and left her a message of what I had done and how I was feeling so bad. She wanted me in the hospital. I wanted to die. I should have gone into the hospital. I hadn't cut myself in three years, and then in a period of thirty-six hours I cut myself four times. I was out of control. It was the only thing that made me feel okay for just an instant. I felt like I immediately needed to kill myself. I counted pills, I contemplated knives, I tried to steal blades . . . I even thought about jumping over the fence onto the highway. I paged Dr. Yamon twice, and I left her about five messages. Both of us were just trying to make it through this hard time. Dr. Fluten was away, and she was the one who usually deals with these emergencies.

"Please take me seriously, I almost killed myself Thursday night, and I can't stop cutting myself." My parents took away my meds and my razors. That did not make me feel better though. I posted a message on the MHN forum online (www.mentalhelp.net) where I spend about an hour each day. I pleaded for help. I asked for someone to respond to me. I needed friends, yet I didn't have anyone I trusted enough to reach out and call.

I received fifteen E-mails and about ten replies on the board to my post. I felt *so* guilty for making these innocent people worry about me. But it felt so good to have some friends. One woman talked to me on AIM for an hour while I tried to gather the courage to page Dr. Yamon. Several people e-mailed me their phone numbers and asked me to call. My life has been revolving around these forums ever since I got diagnosed; yet I never really posted about myself. I just answered people's questions. That night though, I couldn't stop myself, and I felt so supported.

By the end of the weekend the thoughts that I needed to kill myself were settling down; the crisis was coming to an end. I still felt like I wanted to die, and if I had the chance, I would have. However, the crisis was over, and I felt a little calmer.

Now I've written this book, *Growing Up with Psychosis: A Memoir.* I wanted this book to come to a happy end. Unfortunately my life may not have a happy ending. It will always be a struggle. Some times will be easier than others, but I will always be fighting. Most things are harder for me because I grew up so isolated in my own world. I used to hate therapy, but now I kind of like it; I am learning so much. I have to be careful to take things slowly because although one day I will do something that means something to someone, for now I am just learning to take care of myself. I wanted to be a doctor. I had to face reality that right now I am not ready to go to medical school. With only a few hours of sleep a night I would be a mess, more so than the average student. I have not given up hope though that after a few years working as a teacher or an artist or a therapist, I will have the ability and strength to go to medical school. Maybe, maybe not. It's not worth giving up hope.

EPILOGUE

After completing her book, Brooke spent the summer of 2001 working in a bookstore. When she returned to school that fall, the stress of the events of September 11, 2001, and of several other pressures resulted in her being admitted to an inpatient ward for two weeks where she underwent yet another medication change. Since October 4, 2001, she has been out of the hospital, and since then we have had the pleasure, as parents, of watching Brooke succeed on many fronts.

As an athlete, for example, in 2002 she made it through an entire season of lacrosse at Brandeis University, and we watched in amazement as she was named Most Valuable Player by her teammates. As a student, she earned top grades at Brandeis and was named to the National Society of Collegiate Scholars. Her academic success gave her the confidence to apply and eventually to be accepted for a program in nursing at Simmons College where she is moving closer to her goal of a career in medicine helping others.

Brooke has also succeeded in her effort to be more forthright and public about her circumstances. Writing this book was certainly an important first step. Since then, Brooke has demanded and received reasonable accommodations for her illness at her school. She has allowed McLean Hospital to feature her story in some of their press releases and publications. She awed us when she stood up and gave a remarkable speech on her illness to several hundred medical professionals that resulted in a standing ovation.

We are often asked how we were able to get through all these so far and what allowed us to survive as a family. In addition to a great deal of good fortune, we believe that the key strengths that worked for us were the incredible courage of our daughter, the love and support of our two sons, and some remarkable medical professionals who were not only competent but caring. In addition, the good wishes and prayers of our friends and even of some strangers were necessary counterbalances to the stresses we have undergone.

In our world, there has been for too long a stigma attached to mental illness. We hope that Brooke's willingness to share her story will inspire others to talk about mental illness. We have learned that mental illness does not have to be a terminal condition, and the mentally ill do not always have to be confined permanently to locked wards. With luck, this lesson will inspire others to fight for proper treatment for themselves and their loved ones. We consider ourselves to be the most fortunate people on this earth and hope that others can realize some of the joy that we have gotten from our experience.

Frank and Elise Katz

Printed in the United States
67532LVS00002B/40-42